Arranging Music for Young Players

Philippe Oboussier

Arranging Music for Young Players

a handbook on basic orchestration

Oxford University Press
Music Department, 44 Conduit Street, London W1R 0DE

ISBN 0   19   321495   4

© Oxford University Press 1977

Contents

Abbreviations and conventional signs

INSTRUMENTS

bar	= baritone	fl	= flute	t.hn	= tenor horn
B.D.	= bass drum	glock	= glockenspiel	timp	= timpani
bn	= bassoon	gt	= guitar	tbn	= trombone
ch.b	= chime bar(s)	hn	= horn	tpt	= trumpet
cl	= clarinet	ob	= oboe	tri	= triangle
cor a	= cor anglais	pf	= pianoforte	va	= viola
cym	= cymbal	picc	= piccolo	vc	= cello
db	= double bass	rec	= recorder	vn	= violin
euph	= euphonium	S.D.	= side-drum	xylo	= xylophone

SIGNS

1°	= primo = first player	V = up-bow
2°	= secondo = second player	∩ = down-bow
a 2	= both players	LH = left hand
		RH = right hand

ITALIAN TERMS

arco = bowed strings	pizz = pizzicato = plucked strings
colla = with the... (ie play the	trem = tremolo
(col) same part as...)	unis = unisono = in unison
div = divisi = divided	

LETTERED PITCH

Helmholtz's system has been adopted for use:

Introduction

Recent developments in music have rendered traditional notation and
standard instrumental techniques unserviceable. However, most youngsters
want to perform music which bears some relation to their early musical
experience and to the basic elements of melody, rhythm and texture. This
book is not concerned with the avant-garde. What it does attempt to do
is to provide practical help to the teacher - whether in training or in
service - who is frequently called upon to provide music for young instrumentalists, often in heterogeneous groups such as the 'fiddle, cello, big
bass drum; bassoon, flute and euphonium' of the Cornish Furry Dance.
And while in some ways it is easy to write for the professional musician,
for whom the technical problems are few, it is quite another matter to
know what is possible and musically effective for a second-year fiddler or
the beginner brass ensemble.

The technical standard assumed in this book does not go above about Grade 5
of the Associated Board of the Royal Schools of Music. Sections deal with
instruments individually, in family groups, and in mixed groups. Also considered are those instruments associated with music in junior schools -
recorders, guitars, violins, and tuned and untuned percussion of various
kinds.

Suggestions for the preparation of scores and individual parts and the
duplicating of material are made in the hope that they may help to provide
teachers and their students with clear, precise instructions which will
save valuable rehearsal time and further a better musical result.

Success in politics has been called 'the art of the possible'. It requires
both instinct and craft. So too does the successful ordering of musical
materials, whether in original composition or in arranging existing music.
The composer or arranger for instrumentalists of limited technique requires
a basic knowledge of how instruments work, why young players will manage
this phrase but not that one, and why, when pizzicato is indicated, it
won't be forthcoming if insufficient time has been allowed for the player
to get his finger to the string. And he will be the first to comment on
the impossibility of the instruction! So, 'the art of the possible'.
Overcoming all the technical problems is a craft; one hopes that there
will still remain some artistic instinct to produce a musical result.

We are grateful to the following publishers for permission to reproduce
short extracts from music which is their copyright, as follows:

Boosey and Hawkes Music Publishers Ltd. (Bartók: Concerto for Orchestra;
    Stravinsky: Pulcinella Suite).
Novello & Company Ltd. (Elgar: Enigma Variations).
Peters Edition, London, Frankfurt and New York (Strauss, R.: Don Quixote).
The Royal Musical Association (Locke: Suite no 6: Sarabande).

ACKNOWLEDGEMENTS
I wish to thank the following for valuable technical advice: John and
Margaret Farnon, and David Price, of Dauntsey's School; Sandra Rawlings
and David Stanley, of St Luke's College, Exeter; Victor Webber, of Rolle
College, Exmouth. Without the editorial expertise of Sally Wright and,
above all, without the skills and patience of Angela Day, who typed the
final script, this book would have remained in an unintelligible and
illegible form. I am most grateful to both ladies.

Topsham, Exeter: September 1976   Philippe Oboussier

Part 1 Chapter I
General problems and approach

It is here assumed that we are talking about arranging, rather than compos-
ing, music for specified instrumental forces of a known technical competence.
What are the questions which the arranger must answer before committing
himself to paper?

CHOICE OF SUITABLE MUSIC

This must relate to the instruments available and their performing standard. For instance, there is a big difference between simplifying for
school orchestra a work originally intended for a professional symphony
orchestra, and arranging a folk song for a junior group of recorders,
guitar, and tuned percussion. Equally, some very simple music, such as
Song No 43 by Orlando Gibbons, used in this book to demonstrate certain
elementary techniques, can suit almost any homogeneous or mixed group of
performers. Other music, especially that which is strongly idiomatic in
terms of the instrument for which it was conceived — for instance the
Baroque violin school and much nineteenth-century piano music — is seldom
transferable to other instruments.

The case studies in this book reflect a wide selection of source material.
There are straight transcriptions of four-part music, expansions from small
to large and reductions from large to small scores, simplified versions and
translations from one medium to another, and free arrangements of given
melodies. Because copyright laws restrict the use of much twentieth-century music as source material, it has fallen to the author to provide a
few 'genre' pieces for the purpose of a particular exercise. See p 10 for
a detailed list of all case studies within the body of the book. Further
suggestions for suitable music may be found on pp 167-70.

KEY AND RANGE

It is most important when considering a piece of music that key and range
are suited to the instruments available. If the key is right — basically
sharp for strings and flat for wind — then the range may be wrong. If the
key is wrong, it can be remedied by transposition and may solve the range
problem at the same time. However, there are many occasions when the two
are incompatible. Suitable keys and ranges will be discussed for each
instrument and for the group situation. Here, particularly in mixed groups,
the choice of key has to be a compromise.

WHAT SORT OF ARRANGEMENT?

Music may be treated variously, depending on its character and style, and
on the potential of the forces for which the arrangement is intended.

Transcription

The easiest type of arrangement is the direct transcription of a simple
piece of music, such as a four-part chorale or hymn tune, for four instruments. The Song by Gibbons will transfer successfully to a brass quartet
of two trumpets, horn and trombone. It so happens that the original key
of F suits the elementary range of all the instruments involved, and here
the only technical complication is transposition: see pp 150-3.

Case Study 1: Song No 46 by Orlando Gibbons

Only the melody and bass line are original. The inner parts in the first
version given below are as found in the English Hymnal, No 98, 'Drop, drop,
slow tears'.

Transcribed for brass quartet, this becomes:

For further examples using this melody, see pp 53 and 104.

Expansion

It is easier to expand a small score than to reduce an orchestral work to
chamber music proportions. Important thematic material can be doubled
(see p 7), more elaborate accompanying figures introduced, and rhythmic
points underlined by percussion and wind.

At this point it is worth looking at what William Byrd did with a simple
tune. Imagine treating 'The Carman's Whistle' as the starting point for
an arrangement. Expansion of the first statement might lead to ideas as
developed by Byrd in his variations. Only the first bar is given of each
version (see p 143).

Reduction

Much orchestral music can be reduced to what is playable by two hands on a
keyboard. When planning an arrangement for smaller forces, it is often
advisable to make a short score transcription, reducing the music to the
bare essentials in the first instance. This will ensure that unnecessary
doublings are omitted, and if the piece requires transposing, the inexperienced arranger will find it easier to do this in the short score form.
From the transposed version, the planned arrangement can be made. In the
Case Study given below, two bars are worked out in the suggested way:

Case Study 2: 'Nimrod' from Enigma Variations by Elgar

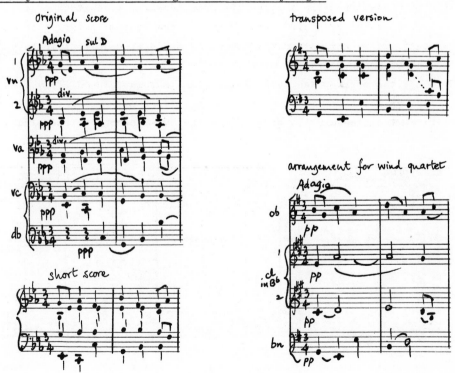

Notice that the key, originally rather low, has been changed to make it
easier for the oboe to play quietly. To achieve a good legato, repeated
crotchets in accompanying parts have been tied and bow marks altered to
suit woodwind. The composer does just this when the wind repeat the theme
in the original score.

Simplification

Often associated with reduction and translation, the simplifying of a score
relates particularly to piano music. Certain keyboard figurations, such as
arpeggios, do not readily suit many other instruments, above all elementary
strings.

Passages like the typical Classical figuration:

may have to be altered to two violins playing:

or upper woodwind playing  and horns

which serves to point up the underlying harmony.

(concert pitch)

Translation

This involves arranging a piece of music for specified instruments, so that
it can be played by a differently constituted group. A very good example
may be found in Mozart's own arrangement for string quintet of the Serenade
in C minor for wind octet, K 388.

Here are the opening ten bars of the first movement, which repay close study,
particularly the off-beat movement of the inner strings in bar 10, which sub-
stitutes the single cello quavers for the two bassoons in the wind version:

Free arrangements

These — for example, accompaniments to given melodies such as folk songs
and dances — need a prior knowledge of basic harmony and a confidence in
handling instruments in a characteristic manner. However, the creative
musician will not be deterred, and provided the melody concerned has certain built-in features such as a simple formal structure and a conventional
tonal outline, it is often easy to provide an adequate and effective accompaniment, possibly based on an ostinato: see p 30 , with a rhythmic ostinato, and all versions of 'We've been awhile a-wandering', where the first
part is always based on an ostinato figure.

For those who cannot easily think in terms of instrumental colour and the
technical and musical problems involved in handling larger groups of
instruments, it is advisable to write a 'short' keyboard score in the first
instance. From this reference score one can expand the material for the
available instrumental forces.

STYLE

Style concerns the suitability of a medium to express a particular musical
idea.

Tonal colour

Much early music does not depend on tonal colour and it can be performed
effectively by a wide variety of instruments. As orchestration developed,
particular instruments and sounds became associated with particular expressive meaning. A typical example is the cor anglais melody at the
beginning of the Largo in Dvořák's Symphony 'From the New World'. On p 77
is a brass ensemble version of this melody, which is given initially to the
horn, an instrument which, like the cor anglais, conveys a feeling of nostal-
gia. Clearly, the trombone would be unsuited to the tune in question. When

assigning a part to an instrument, always try to think in terms of the
resulting sound.

Instrumental character

If tonal colour is one aspect of style which should be respected, then in
a wider sense the arranger must consider whether, for instance, a Chopin
Étude can be adequately performed by instruments other than the piano for
which it was conceived. The sustaining quality of piano tone and the
characteristic pedalled arpeggio passages are almost impossible to reproduce, and music of this strongly idiomatic kind is best avoided as source
material for arranging. It is stylistically unsuitable. Piano music of a
more percussive and rhythmic quality can be considered.

Remember that instruments, in the manner in which they are made and played,
acquire a musical style and character of their own.

Texture

Texture can be thick or transparent, linear or vertical. A highly contrapuntal piece needs clarity of expression which cannot be provided with the
doubling of voices. The heavily orchestrated versions of Bach's organ
fugues are not very successful. On the other hand, a piece in which there
is a basic harmonic accompaniment to one or two melodic strands can be
arranged effectively for large forces. The case studies based on the
carol 'We've been awhile a-wandering' illustrate this type of arrangement.
Consider other problems: for instance, a four-part piece involving a mixture of harmonic and contrapuntal textures. Does one double voices, which
provides a built-in safety factor and may give a sense of security to the
inexperienced performer, or does one alternate phrases between different
blocks of instruments, which allows a breather to those who need it most,
the wind section? Or does one allot one instrument to a part, sharing the
four original lines in turn among perhaps a dozen players? The case study
on pp 118-26 demonstrates possible solutions to this problem.

Balance and blend

In the context of junior and school bands and orchestras, good balance and
blend is more likely to depend on local conditions than on the skills of
the arranger. One has to try to accommodate the ten clarinets and half a
bassoon, giving all the opportunity to play at their respective standards.
Remember that whatever the numerical balance within a group, a number of
factors will influence the tonal spectrum of a score:

a)   some instruments are always louder than others - trombone/viola

b)   some instruments are always more strident than others - oboe/clarinet

c)   high notes are generally more audible than middle or low notes

d)   strings blend well, their tonal characteristics being homogeneous.
     The same may be said of the brass family
e)   the woodwind are individuals and generally have to be treated as such
f)   large numbers of percussion can be devastating: use with discretion
g)   to achieve a chord in which no constituent note predominates, one must
     consider the number of instruments playing each note and the power of
     each instrument related to the register in which it is playing. This
     is no easy matter, and the addition of the correct dynamic marks to
     realise a bland chord is the result of careful listening and long
     experience. It is not always desirable to aim at an equally balanced
     chord. Emphasis on a particular note or group of notes within a
     certain range may be necessary to create the required effect. These
     and other points will be considered in the body of the book.

The problems involved in achieving a sophisticated result are very complex
and one can only refer readers to the scores of great composers and to
treatises which set out to cover the subject more fully: see the Biblio-
graphy.

Doubling

Basic do's and don'ts

   Melodies: It is safe to double at the unison and up an octave. If
   doubling down an octave, beware of writing below the bass line, assuming
   that this itself is not doubling the melody, as in the opening of
   Mozart's Serenade K 388, quoted on p 4.
   Bass line: It is safe to double at the unison and down an octave, as
   with the double bass added to the cello. Do not double up an octave if
   this leads to the bass line crossing above a middle part, so inverting
   the chord. Any bass line doubled up an octave will tend to obscure the
   texture, and this procedure is therefore to be avoided.
   Filler parts: Remember the points discussed on p 6 and above when considering doubling. There is no substitute for the careful study of music
   through listening and looking at scores. If the aim is to produce music
   sounding like Brahms', then look at his scoring, very much thicker in the
   doubling of inner parts than in the clarity of Haydn's writing.

These general remarks will be amplified in the detailed discussion on
instruments and in the comments on case studies.

Expression

Always mark score and parts carefully with the various signs and verbal
instructions which help the player to give a musical performance.

Beyond the choice of suitable tone colour to express a particular mood,
the strengthening of a part by doubling to emphasise a phrase, and other
similar aids to musical expression, there remain a number of devices which
help to make a piece of music sound exciting, relaxing, cheerful or sad.
The crescendo, for example, was used by Beethoven to create tension and
excitement. How was this achieved in orchestral terms? An example from
his 'Eroica' symphony will serve to demonstrate a number of points.   The
extract comes from the first movement, a few bars before the coda.

Notice the gradual
introduction of semi-
quavers: bar 3 violas,
bar 5 both violins and
bar 6 a drum roll,
measured in semi-
quavers. The wind
also become more
active through bars
4 and 5, both in
numbers of instruments
and notes.

It is the repetition
of notes in all depart-
ments of the orchestra
which creates the cres-
cendo and level of ex-
citement. Other factors
working to this end are:
a thickening of texture,
and the wide spread of
high and low notes, as
in bar 5. Notice that
whereas the upper strings
can play semi-quavers,
these are too fast for
single-tongued wind and
the heavier strings.

It is impossible to catalogue here the many possible ways in which composers
have achieved musically expressive effects. The one example given only
emphasises the importance of studying the great composers.

HOW TO USE THE BOOK

This is not a tutor in the accepted sense of the word. There are no
exercises and it is not progressive; that would be well-nigh impossible
with such a complex subject. It is rather a handbook with a comprehensive
index and many cross-references.

It is assumed that a basic knowledge of harmony has been acquired and
there is no discussion of composition techniques used in the free arrangements.

In Chapters II to V the four family groups are discussed. Instruments are
treated individually and associated techniques, such as bowing, are considered in some detail. Family group arrangements in the form of annota-
ted case studies complete each chapter. The varied collection of instruments found in the junior school are treated as a group in Chapter VI.
There follow a series of arrangements for mixed groups, from the small
ensemble to the orchestra and wind bands.

Chapter XII contains a section on transposition and the instruments involved, and guidelines to writing and duplicating music. The select biblio-
graphy is intended as a pointer to further reading. The problems involved
in choosing suitable music have already been enumerated. While the list
of possible sources is necessarily incomplete, it is hoped that the
suggestions made will assist the arranger in his search for interesting
and adaptable scores.

TABLE OF CASE STUDIES, WITH AN ANALYSIS OF THE TYPE OF ARRANGEMENT INVOLVED

No of Case Study	Page number	Title of piece	Composer or source	Instrumental forces required by arrangement	ostinato	transposition	free	simplification	reduction	expansion	translation	transcription
1	2	Song no 46	Orlando Gibbons	brass quartet								x
2	3	Nimrod (Enigma Variations)	Elgar	woodwind quartet		x			x			
3	26	Erinnerung	Schumann	strings				x		x		
4	30	Parson's Farewell	trad	strings			x					
5	32	London Bridge	trad arr JPO	string quartet	x					x	x	
6	44	Magic Flute (extract)	Mozart	clarinet quartet							x	x
7	52	Song no 46	Orlando Gibbons	woodwind quartet							x	x
8	54	Intrada	Pezel	woodwind quintet		x					x	x
9	57	Divertimento (K 213)	Mozart	woodwind quartet		x			x		x	
10	63	Austria (hymn)	Haydn	brass ensemble							x	x
11	75	Branle simple	Attaingnant	brass quartet							x	x
12	77	Largo (Symphony no 9)	Dvořák	brass band ensemble								
13	80	Folk Dance	JPO	brass quartet		x			x	x	x	
14	93	We've been awhile a-wandering	trad carol	junior ensemble		x					x	
15	96	Microdanse: Hommage à B.B.	JPO	junior ensemble	x		x	x	x			
16	104	Song no 46	Orlando Gibbons	small mixed ensemble	x							
17	108	Interlude to carol	trad	small mixed ensemble		x						x
18	110	Helston Furry Dance	JPO	small mixed ensemble								
19	113	We've been awhile a-wandering	trad carol	orchestra	x		x					
20	118	Sarabande (Suite no 6)	Matthew Locke	orchestra	x		x					
21	128	We've been awhile a-wandering	trad carol	brass band			x					
22	132	Entr'acte (Rosamunde)	Schubert	brass band	x					x	x	
23	136	We've been awhile a-wandering	trad carol	wind band	x	x	x			x	x	
24	143	The Carman's Whistle	William Byrd	wind band	x	x	x			x	x	x

Chapter II
Strings: The instruments

FAMILY CHARACTERISTICS

The versatility of string instruments in tonal and dynamic range, in
agility, and above all in the ability to express musical ideas with the
finesse we associate with the human voice, has given the members of the
family a pre-eminent place in instrumental music since the beginning of
the seventeenth century. All the instruments have four strings, tuned as
follows:

Notice that the cello is tuned exactly an octave below the viola, whose
upper three strings are common in pitch to the lower three strings of the
violin. The double bass, whose notes sound an octave lower than written,
does not extend below E, a point to remember when it shares a common bass
line with the cello.

Tone

Within the technical limitations of the elementary player, the quality and
variety of string tone is bound to be restricted. However, a few general
points arise. The top string always sounds brightest, particularly in the
case of the violin, where the string is made of steel. The bottom string,
made of metal wound around gut or steel, is the richest in sonority. This
excerpt from the 'Enigma Variations', where Elgar directs the whole of the
melody to be played 'sul G', or on the lowest string, well demonstrates the
point:

The variety in timbre between the four strings results from the fact that
although they are all of the same length, weight and tension have to be
different in order to produce notes tuned a fifth or a fourth apart. The
longer strings of the larger instruments are also more sonorous. For instance, the open Gs of the cello and double bass sound different even though
at the same pitch, in the same way that a tenor and a bass singing the same
note sound different.

Tone is also affected by the manner and position of bowing. The speed and
pressure of the bow on the strings control more than dynamics. Tone is
quieter and less defined if a string is bowed near the fingerboard. Conversely, the nearer to the bridge, the harder and more penetrating the
sound.

Attack: this is linked to bowing technique, and will be considered in
detail on pp 15-19.

Suitable music
Most music can be arranged for strings. For the inexperienced player, a
number of note patterns are to be avoided, particularly the arpeggio and
Alberti bass figurations found in much keyboard music. These have to be
adapted to suit elementary string technique: see p 25.
For beginners, simple folk melodies, hymn tunes and Renaissance songs and
dances are very suitable: see p 30. The early Baroque provides a rich
repertory, but by the eighteenth century and the music of Haydn and Mozart,
string technique was sufficiently advanced to be beyond the ability of the
inexperienced player.
Idiomatic piano music of the nineteenth century is seldom suitable, though
exceptions can be found among Schumann's children's pieces. The more percussive style of much of today's easy piano music, such as the arrangement
of 'London Bridge' on p 32, can result in effective elementary string
music.

Suitable keys
Open strings and basic fingering determine the easiest and most effective
keys for beginners. Where the advanced player will avoid unfingered open
strings, they are much used at an elementary level, playing in first and
third positions. As a result, G, D, and A major, and A and E minor are the
easiest keys.

ELEMENTS OF STRING TECHNIQUE
Left-hand and bowing techniques must be clearly understood if a part is to
be playable and musically satisfying. The principles apply to all strings
and where there are differences, these will be noted.

Positions : violin
                                    ∧   ∧
The basic finger patterns are: 0 1 23 4 and 0 12 3 4;   o = open string:
1,2,3,4 = LH fingers: ∧ = closed finger position for semitone interval.
The fourth finger is not used by beginners. A two octave scale of G major
demonstrates the use of both basic finger patterns in first position.

Strings are labelled: I(top) E: II A: III D: IV(bottom) G

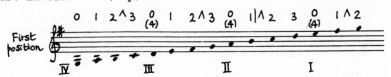

Beginner violinists usually move from first to third position, involving a
shift of the hand up the neck so that the first finger starts a third
higher than previously. A two octave scale of D major demonstrates this
position. Use of the fourth finger is now essential, no open notes being
allowed:

The scale of F major shows the problem which beginners encounter with flat
keys. Here the first finger has to extend back (1) towards the nut for
B flat and, in the first example, for F. Both versions require shifting
from first to third position:

Second and fourth positions may avoid unnecessary crossing of strings.
This tune in B flat major is simple in second position, hardly the case if
it is attempted in the first position:

Positions: viola
As for the violin, with wider spacing between the fingers.

Positions: cello
The basic first position patters is 0 1 3̂4, at which point one moves on to
the next open string:

For further details see pp 22-3.

Positions: double bass

The basic first position pattern is shown
in the G major scale, involving all four
strings. For further details see pp 23-4.

Position charts

Since the writing of easy string music presupposes a knowledge of left-
hand technique, those who are not themselves string players are advised to
make out a chart for each instrument on the pattern of that given here for
the violin.

LH fingerings are given hori-
zontally, and positions below
the bottom string. Positions
and their respective fingerings apply vertically to all
strings. Obviously, any finger
may shift forwards or backwards
a semitone without altering the
basic hand position.

o = octave harmonic, effected
by stopping the string lightly
at half its length.

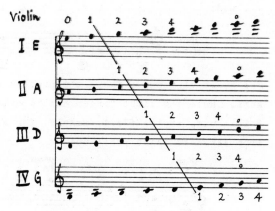

positions   1st 2nd 3rd 4th 5th

Certain deductions can be made from what has been said and from a close
study of the chart:

a) The easiest and most effective keys for strings lie 'on the sharp side'
   of C major and A minor.

b) Rapid and slurred passages which cross strings are to be avoided.
   Inexperienced players deserve any help that can be given in the fingering of tricky passages.

c) Phrases involving notes above the third position should be treated with
   caution.

d) The interval of a fifth (a fourth on the double bass), other than between open strings, involves moving the _same_ finger to the adjacent
   string, or shifting on a single string. Neither alternative is easy at
   speed or if slurred.

e) Double-stopping involves playing a two-note chord on _adjacent_ strings.
   Apart from open-string fifths, it is generally preferable to indicate
   divisi (_div._) — one player to each note.

Unisono (unis.) restores both players at a desk to a single part. The
easiest double-stops are a) one fingered note with one open note and b)
sixths, both notes fingered:

f) If in any doubt, ask a string player for advice. A practical demonstration is the quickest and most effective way of learning about the problems of writing for strings. No amount of theory can be a substitute
   for a live demonstration.

BOWING

The general principles of bowing are common to all string instruments.
Taking into account what is practicable for the elementary player, the aim
is to provide for a musical performance. Insert essential bowings rather
than leaving decisions to the individual. Players need guidance, and it is
easier to alter markings in the light of rehearsal experience than to leave
everything to chance. The bow divides into three parts: point (or tip) —
heel (or frog), where it is held — middle, which, if measured by weight
rather than length, is about a third of the way along from the heel. This
is the easiest part of the bow to control.

Before detailing bow markings and their effect on performance, a few
general principles should be clearly understood:

down-bows	= strong beats	: up-bows	= weak beats
long bows	= long notes	: short bows	= short notes
heavy pressure	= forte	: light pressure	= piano
rapid movement	= forte	: slow movement	= piano

A very simple example serves to demonstrate a few problems related to the
principles outlined above:

Down-bows come on down-beats, up-bows on up-beats — no problems. However,
in the first two bars, the down-bow lasts three times as long as the up-bow,
so that one will 'run out of bow' unless pressure is lightened on the
crotchet, thus avoiding a loud bump as one skates back to the heel for the
next long note. The crotchet E in the second full bar can be played with
more weight because of the crescendo, and it is particularly important to
get back to the heel for the loud third bar, where heavy, long and fairly
rapid bows will be needed, lightening the pressure as one returns to the

heel for the long final note. Even in this short phrase, considerable control will have to be exercised over the bow if the result is to be musical
and faithful to the dynamic markings.

Bow markings

It is important for the arranger to understand the language which indicates
to a string player how a piece of music is to be played. The more elementary bowing techniques and their notation are discussed in relation to
examples designed to illustrate valid musical points.

Where there are no bow marks, the following is assumed:

A phrase starting on a down-beat is taken with a down-bow. This naturally
accentuates the attack, the weight of the bow being 'under the hand'. Any
exception to this convention must be indicated. In the following example,
there are two reasons for starting with an up-bow. The syncopated accent
on the crotchet in bars 1-3 suggests a down-bow, and by starting with an
up-bow, this is achieved in each bar. When leaping at speed from a low to
a high string on the cello this is best done at the heel, thus avoiding a
wide movement of the bow arm. After the first up-bow, an exception to the
general rule given above, no further bow marks are necessary, since alternate bowing (see below) is assumed.

A phrase starting on an up-beat is taken with an up-bow. This allows the
following down-beat to be taken with a down-bow. The melody of 'God Save
the Queen' will be used to demonstrate effects - both technical and musical - resulting from different bow markings. Bow marks within brackets are
inserted to help the reader follow comments made. They are not needed by
the player and would normally be omitted.

Alternate or détaché bowing 'on the string'

This is assumed where no bow marks are inserted. In the example, one
starts with a down-bow and continues bowing alternately up and down to the
end. Bowings have been added to show the result in terms of long and short
strokes, in relation to note lengths and accentuation:

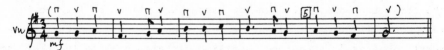

Notice that in triple time alternate bowing gives an up-bow on alternate
strong beats, and in the above case, a down-bow on weak quavers. Though
this bowing is quite possible, it is not very subtle in terms of musical
phrasing.

Slurred bowing

A slur between two or more notes indicates that they are to be played with
one stroke of the bow. The string slur therefore has a very different
meaning from the phrasing slur used in piano music.

Comment: Slurs make it possible to get a down-bow on accented beats:
bars 1,3,5: a down-bow to ♩:an up-bow to ♩♩ helps stress the accent on
the first beat.
bars 2,4: Here we have the opposite effect: a rapid light up-bow on the
third beat is necessary if the player is not to run out of bow by bar 6.
bar 1: To avoid crossing strings under a slur, the 4th finger is advised.

It is already evident that even at a very elementary level, bowing has a
considerable effect on fingering, phrasing, and problems arising from
crossing strings. To illustrate this in more detail, alternative versions
of the second part of the tune will be analysed. But first let us consider
the join from the first
part to the second part:
Comment: bars 5-7: the bowing in bar 5 allows an up-bow in bar 6. This
helps the cresc. to the forte in bar 7, as pressure on the bow is increased
near the heel with an up-bow.

Alternatively one might phrase it:
Comment: Here the bowing allows for emphasis on both down-beats, and
whereas the first bowing would suit an arrangement where wind fill in
in bar 6, this version is more suited to accompany voices.
The bow lift between two down-bows synchronizes with a breath mark.

We will now consider the last ten bars of 'God Save the Queen':

Comment: bars 7-10: forte requires full alternate bowing.
bars 11-13: the slurs are added to allow a down-bow on down-beats and an
up-bow on cresc. to the climax in bar 13. This avoids crossing strings
under a slur and the need to use the 4th finger.

An alternative version might be phrased:

Comment: The bowing here emphasizes the two-bar sequence suggested by:

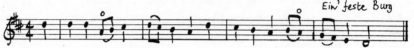

Where in triple time there can be problems with alternate bowing, as the analysis of 'God Save the Queen' has shown, these largely disappear in duple time:

Comment: Apart from the slurred quavers, no bow marks are necessary according to convention: see p 16. Notice the string crossing <u>between</u> pairs of slurred quavers if A is played on an open string.

Staccato bowing

There are several different types of staccato bowing. Apart from individual notes, a group may be played staccato within a slur:

Comment: Here in bar 1 we have a genuine staccato, the bow stopping between quavers on the string, that is, without lifting the bow. In bar 2, the crotchets are taken in one bow, on the string, the bow again stopping between notes. This type of staccato is easiest on an up-bow, as in the example quoted from Beethoven's Symphony No 7.

The interrupted slur is a more legato form of group staccato, known as <u>louré</u> bowing. It involves the bow almost stopping between notes: a typical example comes from the introduction to 'Comfort ye' in Handel's 'Messiah':

Common rhythmic patterns in Baroque music such as and are usually
bowed or (=), and (=). In certain cases the semi-
quaver may be shortened: and . Handel's 'Messiah' provides many
examples of these forms of group staccato:

written

performed

Spiccato

Used for light accompaniments in fast music, spiccato bowing, played with
alternate up- and down-bows at the middle, is indicated with staccato dots.
It is only suitable for music marked <u>p</u> to <u>mf</u>:

Other bowings

a) <u>Emphasis</u>: for strong emphasis, take successive down-bows where poss-
    ible, as in bar 1 — but not in bar 3, where there is insufficient time:

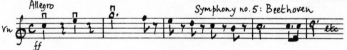

b) For light accompaniments,
    take successive up-bows,
    especially in off-beat
    patterns as in Schubert's
    Rosamunde music:
    (Entr'acte no 2)

c) Changing bows within a long note is often necessary in loud passages,
    particularly for the shorter-bowed cello and double bass. Changes
    should be marked away from strong beats:

 rather than

Tremolo

a) A measured tremolo is an 'on the string' version of spiccato: see
    p 19. It is particularly effective in quiet passages:

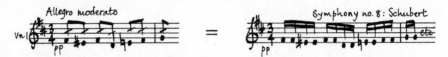

The number of lines drawn above or through the tail of a note determines the exact number of notes to be played.

b) Unmeasured tremolo produces a quiet shimmering effect and is notated:

c) Fingered tremolos between two notes on one string are best avoided at
    this stage.

Trills and turns must be playable on **one** string.

Pizzicato : arco

In any rapid change, arrange for an up-bow before and a down-bow after **pizz**.
Remember that it does take time to change.

Mutes (con sord: senza sord)

Allow ample time for putting on and taking off mutes. Although muting
makes it easier to play quietly, the important musical effect is a veiling
of the tone colour. It is advisable not to score for mutes for beginners.
Double bass muting is impracticable.

Summary

The foregoing section has been designed to help the non-string-player.
The best way to learn how to write well for elementary strings is to start
playing one of the instruments. Even a modicum of skill will ensure practicable fingering and bowing.

THE INSTRUMENTS

VIOLIN

Characteristics

Equally effective as a melody or accompanying instrument. In standard four-
part string writing violins are divided into firsts and seconds. The latter
may double the melody in unison or at the lower octave, or act as the alto
to the firsts' soprano. The violin is the most agile and flexible member of
the string family.

Range

The upper limit depends on the player's ability
to finger notes in high positions. Generally
speaking, do not stray beyond third position;
however, by sliding the fourth finger up to
touch the octave harmonic on the E string, the
range can be extended by one note. For higher
positions see p 14.

<u>Fingering</u> has been discussed on pp 12-13.

VIOLA

Characteristics

The viola varies in size more than other string instruments and youngsters
will inevitably have to match arm and hand to a suitable instrument. At
junior level, where violas tend to be scarce, the part may be played on a
violin strung with A, D and G strings to I, II and III, adding a viola C
as the fourth string.[1] A viola bow is slightly shorter and heavier than
the violin's, and the thicker strings do not sound as bright as those of
the violin. The viola is thus more suited to slower melodic material and
accompanying figurations, at least for the less advanced player. The low
C string, the only one below violin range, overlaps the cello's D string.
The quality of tone is markedly different; it is less rounded. This is
well illustrated by Elgar's use of the instrument in his <u>Enigma Variations</u>:

Range and notation

The alto or viola clef ♭ is standard, except
where an extended part in third position on the
A string makes the treble clef more sensible.
Do not change clefs for the odd high note.

Fingering

As for the violin, but the extra stretch makes a strong fourth finger
essential, and frequent extensions in first position are tiring. It is
difficult to play above third position, since the shoulder of the viola
gets in the way of the left hand.

---

[1]All steel strings are recommended and a Magini model violin with a $14\frac{1}{2}$
inch back (recognized by its double purfling) is very suitable.

CELLO

Characteristics

Normally the bass instrument of the string family, the cello is nevertheless capable of a wide tessitura which makes it a successful solo instrument, either on its own or within the orchestra. Its long strings give a
rich tone; the A string has a particularly fine quality.

The following melody from the second movement of Schubert's 'Unfinished'
Symphony hardly moves out of first position, yet it demonstrates the singing quality of the cello:

Played pizzicato, the cello provides
a light and rhythmical accompaniment
to other instruments, as in the same
movement of the Schubert symphony
quoted above:

Range and notation

The bass clef is used unless an extended
passage high on the A string makes the
tenor clef ♯ more convenient.

Fingering

The wide stretch required in first position must be considered when writing
for elementary players. Standard finger patterns starting on the open
string are:

Arrows show forward and backward extensions. After first position, the
beginner will normally learn to play in fourth position, giving a complete
scale on each open string, the last note being the harmonic octave. The
higher up the string, the smaller the finger stretch between notes. Cellists therefore learn — or should learn —
to move freely over the fingerboard at an
early stage, particularly on the A string:

Because of the wide finger stretch on the cello, some passages which involve
extensions in first position are made easier if the whole hand is moved back
into the half position:

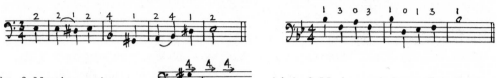

The following notes:    which fall in easy keys for the
violin require an extended fourth finger on the cello, and when approached
from the string above they are liable to be
played flat. It is important to keep this
in mind when writing for beginner cellists:

Bowing

Changes have to be more frequent as the bow is shorter than that of the
violin or viola.

DOUBLE BASS

Characteristics

The main function of this instrument is to double the bass line. The
strengthening of the harmonic bass notes at the lower octave by even one
double bass gives a solidity and fullness of sound which is perhaps more
evident when the instrument stops playing for a few bars. Indeed, it is
important to realize that for the sake of contrast the bass line must at
times be lightened, either by leaving out the double bass or by directing
it to play pizzicato while the cello plays arco: see p 33.
Played with a short, heavy and somewhat stiff bow, the double bass tends
to have a rough tone in the lower finger positions. The fitting of all-
metal strings does facilitate playing, especially for the young. The great
string length and the tuning at an interval of a fourth means frequent
shifts and much string crossing. At an elementary level, a simplified version of the bass line is often necessary:

In view of this, and in spite of the tradition of writing cello and bass parts on the
same line, it is advisable to give each
instrument a separate stave. On its own
the double bass does not provide an adequate bass line and since instruments
and players tend to be scarce, cover the part elsewhere to avoid the risk of
having no bass line at all.

Range

sounding an octave lower than
the written notes

Clefs are as for the cello, but only the bass clef should be used for
elementary players. Because the double bass does not extend to low C,
notes below E must be transposed up an octave if doubling the cello or any
other part. This should be done with respect for the musical line:

this line ——→
is preferable to
this line ——→

Fingering

In the lower positions, the third finger is not used separately. It is
usually placed alongside the fourth finger to give added strength. This
fingering is given as 4 in the basic positions, here starting on the open
top G string:

The scale of D major would therefore be:

Bowing

The bow is short, and heavy pressure is required to get the string into
vibration. Compared with all other string instruments, the double bass
demands more frequent bow changes, particularly on long pedal notes: see
p 19, c).

Arranging for strings

It is only in recent years that the dominance of the string family within
the orchestra has been challenged. Since they do not experience the problem of fatigue associated with the wind family, strings can play, over a
period of time, a greater dynamic and expressive range than any other
group of instruments. Tonally they blend well together and are capable of
producing a great variety of musical sounds, resulting from different bowing techniques, double-stopped chords, various forms of pizzicato, harmonics, and other special effects. At an elementary playing level, however,
the string family poses problems for the composer and arranger which demand
a close understanding of basic string techniques, already discussed on
pp 11-24. We are here concerned with the problems of the string group.

The string family

Assuming a four-part texture, whether harmonic or contrapuntal or a mixture
of both, the normal disposition of strings is:

> violin 1 (S)   violin 2 (A)   viola (T)   cello (B)

with a double bass to reinforce the cello at the lower octave. The spacing
between the parts, particularly in traditional harmonic music, should
generally follow that favoured by voices:

A Bach Chorale, or any well-written piece of vocal music, will illustrate
the point.

For a string band of some 16 players, a good disposition would be:

> vn 1 - 6 players : vn 2 - 4 players : va - 2 players
>
> vc - 3 players : db - 1 player

Part-writing

Traditionally, violin 1 plays the melody, cello and double bass the bass
line, while violin 2 and viola fill in the harmony. This will be demonstra-
ted in 'Parson's Farewell' (see p 30). Paradoxically, the most able
players are usually assigned to the top part, which, though exposed and

musically the most important line, is not necessarily the most difficult.
The tremolo and arpeggio types of 'filler' part so beloved of the great
classical composers can lie very awkwardly across the strings, and care
must be taken to write easy yet effective inner parts for the more elementary player. Otherwise performing ability should be spread equally between first and second violins. It is also a mistake to expect the young
double bass player to move with the agility of a cellist, and a simplified
part should be supplied.

In music where melodic material is shared between the parts, life is
usually more interesting, and even a simple dance like 'Parson's Farewell'
or 'London Bridge' can be arranged so that the viola or cello has part of
the tune.

CASE STUDIES
Some of the problems which have to be considered when arranging for strings
are highlighted in the following examples. The first, originally for piano,
emphasizes how typical pianistic figurations must be translated into simple
string language. The second is a traditional dance tune. The arrangement
is conceived in terms of strings, and does not depend on a piano version as
the original source. The last piece is an example in a more modern idiom.

Case Study 3: 'Erinnerung' ('Reminiscence') from Album for the Young op 68
by Schumann
This volume of piano music has been much explored for exercises in orchestration. Here are the first four bars of the original:

A straight transcription for strings might be:

What is wrong with this?

Key

Is A major suitable? It is certainly possible, but G major would make
everything easier, avoiding G sharp in violin 1, and simplifying the cello
part, not least to avoid the extended fingerings, C sharp and G sharp.

Bowing

The arranger has adopted the generalized piano phrasing slurs. Obviously
these must be altered to indicate bowing. As shown, violin 1 and cello
could manage the 'piano' slurs only by using very little bow to a note,
and thus playing very quietly, quite apart from the difficulty of crossing
strings. This problem is particularly acute in the cello part where, in
first position, the first finger would have to move on adjacent strings
from A to E in bar 1, and the third finger likewise in bar 2; there is also
the added problem of the G sharp extension.

Double-stopping

In bar 3, the D and A are on adjacent open strings (violin 2) and this is
possible, but in first position A and B are on the same string and therefore cannot be played together; it is very difficult to finger the A with
the fourth finger on the D string and the B with the first finger on the A
string. The viola part in bar 3 can stand, since D is an open note. An
up-bow for the viola is required at the start of this bar in order to play
the double-stop on a down-bow. Generally speaking, double-stops are taken
on a down-bow in the early stages. Here, this is even more important in
view of the advisability of finishing on a down-bow.

Fingering

Bar 2, violin 1: the A should be played with the fourth finger on the D
string, to be followed by G sharp, so avoiding crossing from an open string
under a slur; this fingering should be written in.

Pizz/arco

Insufficient time has been allowed for the double bass change in bar 4.
And does ♪ℾ♪ℾ really convey anything different from ♩ ♩ ?

Dynamics

Only violin 1 has been marked p. Each part should be fully marked, including ◁▭ ▭▷ where necessary.

Harmony

The piano arpeggios disguise the basic harmony notes in bars 1 and 2. Look
carefully at the second half of each of these bars and work out the fundamental bass line. Is the double bass part correct in the last bar?

It should by now be evident that this arrangement is unsatisfactory. The
following version attempts to overcome the problems involved:

Key

The change to G major has overcome the problems outlined above.

Bowing

All parts are now bowed according to the principles outlined on pp 15-20.
Strictly it is not necessary to mark the first notes in violin 1 and cello,
but violin 2 and viola should be bowed to avoid confusion. Generally up-
beats are on up-bows, which have a 'built-in' crescendo: study violin 1
for this effect, especially in bar 3. The opposite effect results from a
down-bow; a good attack followed by a fade, as in bars 2 and 4. Violin 1
will have to lighten the pressure on the up-bow at the end of bar 1, having
just played three notes on the down-bow. Other bowings are of course

possible, but notice how towards the end of the example where there is an obvious general crescendo, bows move more frequently, so that the performers can play more loudly.

Double-stopping

These are permissible when they are simple to execute and when they assist in making the texture thicker and the music louder, or when an essential harmony note would otherwise not be present. But they are unnecessary in this extract.

Fingering

Help has been given in the viola part to avoid crossing strings. Fingerings should be treated as aids to a musical performance, and pianists are reminded that 1 indicates the forefinger and not the thumb!

Pizz/arco

No changes are necessary in this short passage. Always allow time to make a change, and if time is short, a pizz should be preceded by an up-bow and succeeded by a down-bow. Remember to indicate changes clearly.

Dynamics

All parts are marked in detail, adding extra indications to ensure a more musical result. Remember that each player has only his own part in front of him, not the full score.

A few further comments arise from this case study:
The music is marked Molto cantabile, and the LH piano part is partially pedalled. It is important that in the arrangement the character of the music is retained, and that pianistic features are translated into string terms. For example, the pedalled LH arpeggios, easy for a pianist, do not readily transfer to strings, since they involve crossing strings with slurred bowing. The second version attempts to overcome this problem in two ways: 1) by breaking up the arpeggios so that they can be played on one string, as in the viola, and by sharing the notes making up an arpeggio between two or more instruments, as in bar 1; and 2) by the combination of a legato cello part and the plucked double bass, whose long strings will sustain the tone. There is therefore no point in writing ♪ 7 ♪ 7 , the effect of which suggests stopping the string vibrating after a quaver. Hence the crotchets in the second version.

In the first version Schumann's chords were transcribed literally, resulting in unmusical inner parts. In the second version, an attempt has been made to make vertical and horizontal aspects of the score read logically in four real parts.

Case Study 4: 'Parson's Farewell'

This dance tune, Flemish in origin but included in John Playford's 'The
Dancing Master' from 1651, is here the subject for an arrangement for first
position strings. The original is in D minor, but when transposed up a
tone the tune lies easily under the fingers (mainly on the E string).
The implied harmony has been added below. This might serve well as the
basis for a guitar accompaniment, but translation to strings requires
attention to rhythmic patterns which will enliven the texture and let in
some air, while providing adequate support at cadences, modulations, and
other points of interest.

In the arrangement below it will be seen that from bars 1 - 8, the harmonic
bass is lightly sketched while violin 2 and viola give a rhythmic ostinato.
From bars 9 - 16, the inner parts join together, while the cello becomes
busier towards the high point of the tune at bar 15. For variety's sake,
the harmony has been extended to include passing dissonances. These are
sometimes unprepared and unresolved, and result from maintaining rhythmic
and melodic sequential phrases.

In bars 14 and 15 the viola overlaps violin 2, not because in this instance
the viola cannot continue down the scale, but because if it did the
spacing of the parts would be unsatisfactory, with the tune high and dry
above its accompaniment. In its turn, violin 2 climbs back above the
viola, allowing the final cadence a well-spaced chord. In a piece of
this kind, avoid the typical layout of a pub pianist's rendering - tune
in the right hand and chordal clusters at the bottom.

Only essential bowings have been added, and the double bass is optional.
In bar 12 it would have to take the higher D. The part is not difficult
and might sound well if played pizzicato.

PARSON'S FAREWELL   from Playford's 'The Dancing Master' 1651

It might be more in-
teresting if the re-
peated second half
were varied by giving
the melody to the
viola and/or the
cello, while violins
add comment above.

In the version given below, notice that the bowing of the tune is different
from that suggested for the violin, where the part is all on one string —
if the open E is used. This is not the case with the lower instruments,
where string-crossing occurs on pairs of quavers. Alternate bowing is
therefore suggested.

Case Study 5: London Bridge

This short piano piece is based on the two tunes associated with the nur-
sery rhymes 'London Bridge is broken down' and 'London Bridge is falling
down'. They are marked A and B in the piano score. Typical of many pieces
written for young pianists, where the melody is shared between left and
right hands, it nevertheless poses a rhythmical problem in the last eight
bars, where the two tunes, one in simple and one in compound time, appear
simultaneously.

GENERAL PRINCIPLES

The first 24 bars present a melody accompanied by chords in from two to
four parts. Assuming that one instrument will play the melody, the other
three can share out the chords, some of which will have to be expanded (or
reduced) to three notes. Notes in a chord must lie within the span of a
young pianist's hand. In an instrumental arrangement this limitation on
spacing need not apply, and chords can be spread out to suit the range of
individual instruments. Every effort should be made to share out the melodic interest between the four instruments. If possible, the viola part
should be written so that it can be played by a third violin in the absence
of a viola player.

The key sequence is unusual - bars 1-8, D major: bars 9-16, A major,
plunging into F major at bar 17 and back to D major for the last 9 bars.
The A major section should therefore be reserved for the violin, an instrument more suited to 'sharp' keys than the viola and cello. The F major section, where the tune is in the left hand, lies well for the cello.

THE ARRANGEMENT

Style and texture

In such a short piece it is desirable that all players should be involved,
and the original version has therefore been reorganized to provide four
parts throughout. Notice particularly the addition of harmony notes in the
viola line in bars 26-31, where the piano version is only in three parts —
two melodies over a pedal bass. Until these last few bars the accompaniment is purposely light. If a double bass were to be available, then a
very simple open string part could be added to underline the cello in bars
9-16 and from 26 to the end.

In the event of the viola part having to be played by a third violin, then
only from the second note in bar 25 to the end would it be necessary to
transpose the line up an octave. The reason it has been kept down here is
to allow the violin 2 tune — originally an octave lower in the piano version — to stand clear of the accompaniment.

Dynamics

In the original the pianist can see the whole score and should therefore be
able to assess the relative importance of the musical elements which make
up a piece. The instrumentalist has only his own part and a pair of ears
to help him gauge the value of his contribution to the whole. Graded dynamics have therefore been added to the arrangement to encourage a light
accompaniment to the melody. Compare the string version with the original.
In the first 24 bars, the melody is marked up, particularly so where the
viola has the opening tune in a tenor range. Whereas in the piano score
the melody was on top in this section, the expansion to four-note chords
has necessitated placing the top two notes in each chord above the tune.
Whenever this arises, it is very important to lighten the accompanying texture. The plucked strings in bars 1-8 should help to project the tune.

TECHNICAL POINTS

Fingering

All parts are in the first position. The second violin part is particularly
easy to play.

Bowing

Melody A (bars 1-8, viola: bars 26 to the end, violin 1): as shown, alternate bowing is prescribed with the exception of the semi-quavers in bars
7 and 31. For more advanced players, a group staccato (see pp 18-19) may
be used:

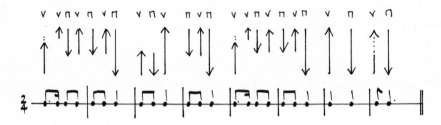

Melody B (bars 9-16, violin 1: bars 17-24, cello: bars 25-33, violin 2):
by starting with an up-bow and bowing détaché near the heel, the right
musical effect should be achieved, ending the eight-bar phrase with a down-
bow:

'Off-the-beat' accompanying chords are best played with successive up-bows
(see p 19), while alternate bowing is suitable for 'on-the-beat' strokes.
Notice the down-bows at the change from pizzicato to arco in bar 8 (see
p 20), and the subsequent up-bows at the beginning of bar 9. To emphasize
the cello's pedal D in the last 8 bars, successive down-bows are suggested.
Bow markings have been inserted only where they are essential, or where any
element of doubt may arise.

SUMMARY

The most important factors to consider in making an arrangement for strings
are:

a) When choosing music, make sure that it will sound characteristic of
   string writing. See pp 167-8 for source material.
b) Transpose to a convenient key - for violins sharp keys are easiest.
   Viola and cello can play in one flat without difficulty.
c) Bowing and fingering must be practicable.

LONDON BRIDGE

Chapter III
Woodwind: The instruments

<u>FAMILY CHARACTERISTICS</u>

The woodwind are agile and school players tend to be technically more advanced than string players. They are therefore well equipped to play an
important part in any mixed ensemble or orchestra. It is well to remember
this, as our heritage in orchestral music leans heavily on the string section being given the most important place in any mixed ensemble. One only
has to think of the Baroque orchestra of Handel or of a Haydn symphony,
where woodwind are used extensively to double a string part, rather than
the reverse.

<u>Tone</u>

The varied tonal characteristics of individual members of the family suit
them to being used as soloists within a group. They do not necessarily
blend together as a choir. Flutes and clarinets, whose tone is generally
smooth, sound well with each other. Likewise oboes and bassoons blend,
having a much richer tonal spectrum allied to the 'edge' of a double reed.
One example is the first Trio in Bach's 'Brandenburg' Concerto no 1.
Bassoons in their tenor register and clarinets in their lower octave make
good partners.

<u>Attack</u>

A note beginning a phrase is 'tongued'. It is possible to make a hard or
a soft attack. Notes can be slurred, though certain progressions can be
very difficult, if not impossible. Wide leaps, particularly downward
leaps, are not easy to slur. Repeated notes must, of course, be tongued.
Mozart's opera <u>The Magic Flute</u> is rich in fine writing for the woodwind,
and this excerpt from the Overture is a good example of crisp repeated
tonguing, here assisting the rhythmic momentum of the piece:

The combination of soft attack and slurring underlines the gentle cantabile
character of the 'March of the Priests' from the same opera:

Suitable music

For elementary players, the music must be kept within defined ranges appropriate to each instrument. These will be discussed under each instrument.
Generally chordal music suits well, such as can be found in collections of
Renaissance dances. The extensive wind music of Mozart includes movements
which can be arranged for instruments less exotic than the basset horn,
and his Divertimenti and Serenades are worth exploring. No piece should
be long, for young players soon become fatigued unless adequate rests are
written into the music. These and other points will be further argued on
pp 50-59.

Suitable keys

The construction of each member of the woodwind family largely determines
the most suitable keys for individual instruments. With the fingering LH:
thumb + 1-2-3 ; RH 1-2-3-4 (that is, as for the bottom note of a recorder),
the flute and oboe play C, the bassoon F, and the clarinet, owing to the
fact that, unlike the others, it overblows at the twelfth rather than at
the octave, plays written F in the lower register and C in the upper register. There is a further complication about the clarinet resulting from it
being a transposing instrument. The B♭ clarinet, with which we are here
concerned, sounds a tone lower than the written note, so that it actually
plays E♭ and B♭. See pp 150-1: Transposition.

If woodwind are to play comfortably together, it is therefore important to
choose keys which are convenient for all participants. Obviously, the
clarinet will always be playing from a part with two more sharps or two
less flats than the others — G major would mean a written part in three
sharps for the clarinet. It is therefore wise to avoid writing in 'concert'
(sounding) keys of more than one, or at the most, two sharps if clarinets
are involved. This raises particular problems in combining the clarinet
with strings, who, in elementary stages, are certain to be confined to
sharp keys. However, other woodwind find F or B♭ comfortable, and it is
noticeable that Mozart in his wind music confined himself almost wholly to
B♭, E♭, and their relative minor equivalents.
In Mozart's works for clarinet and strings or orchestra, both in the key of
A, he of course stipulates an A clarinet, so that in effect the solo part
is written in C major, while the strings are happy in A major.

As brass instruments are built either in B♭, E♭, or in the case of the orchestral horn, F, good keys for wind band forces are the same as for clarinet and other woodwind: flat keys.

THE INSTRUMENTS

FLUTE

Characteristics

This is the purest sounding member of the family. As will be seen from the comments below, there are real problems for the beginner in producing a strong tone at the bottom of the instrument. As this is the area in which it is difficult for the young oboist not to make a lot of noise, the arranger must take care to write in the second register if the flute is to be heard in a leading position. It is no use arranging a hymn tune from the book (SATB) in the usual 'score' order. The oboe's alto line will drown the flute's soprano. See p 42 for further discussion on this point.

The flute is a flexible instrument, and can play rapid passages more easily than the other woodwind. However, compared with the oboe and bassoon, it is not as forceful in attack, except in its top register. The lowest notes are slow to speak, and rapid tonguing will be ineffective below about g' in the bottom octave.

Beginners tend to waste a lot of breath and rapidly run out in playing, so that it is unwise to write long slurred passages. Low notes require more breath than high ones and forte playing is also more demanding on the lungs than piano. If you can sing a passage in one breath, it can probably be managed on the flute in one breath.

Range

The complete range of the flute is:

The beginner's range is:    Additional notes up to
high g''' should be
achieved in the first
two years:

Finger patterns are almost identical for the first two octaves, while the
third octave requires cross fingering. For many beginners it is easier to
play in the second octave than in the first, and it is a mistake to think
that the lowest notes are the simplest.

Do's and don't's
Of these two tunes from The Magic Flute, one is effective, the other not:

Comment: the range is good and the articulation suitable.

Comment: the pitch is too low to project as a solo. It is in fact a vocal
part.
Certain progressions lying 'across the break', when many fingers have to
move to effect stepped or small intervals, are difficult to play in any
rapid passages, particularly when slurred:

Avoid wide slurred leaps, especially in a downward direction. Remember
that the flute requires a lot of breath, especially for low loud notes.
In other ways - embouchure and breathing muscles - it is less fatiguing
to play than the remaining woodwind.

Tuning: even allowing for a well-taught and aurally sensitive player,
some notes are difficult to play in tune. The worst note on the instrument is ♯ which will inevitably be sharp, and will sound particularly so when not enharmonically the leading note in D major.

OBOE
Characteristics
Compared with the flute, the oboe has a penetrating and pungent tone,
strong at the bottom end of the range and becoming thinner as the pitch
rises. Indeed, it is difficult to play quietly from the low b♭ up to about
f', and above g'' young players will find trouble in controlling pitch and
tone. However, in its best range, the oboe can be very expressively played,
though the control over breath and embouchure required to achieve the
necessary tonal flexibility takes some time to develop, and it is unwise
to expect too much finesse from the young player.

As it is impossible to start a note without a tongued attack, it follows
that the oboe, like the bassoon, is capable of excellent sforzato and
staccato playing. The dry pointing of a tongued note will add bite and
clarity of rhythm to any woodwind or string passage:

tutti strings,
obs & bns
in unison

The Magic Flute
Mozart

Rapid articulation is very effective, particularly on repeated notes in
the middle and upper registers. The lowest notes do not, however, respond
kindly either to hard or to rapid tonguing. Much depends on the reed: in
tone quality, in responsiveness to articulation, and in intonation, reeds
vary a great deal, and one of the greatest problems faced by the young
player is the selection and care of reeds. But this is only one of his
problems. The oboe uses up far less air than any other wind instrument,
since very little is able to escape from the lungs through the narrow slit
between the blades of the reed. As a result the oboist is constantly
holding back air, which puts the breathing and neck muscles under some
strain, as well as the musculature around the lips, which have to hold the
reed and act as a seal between oboe and player. It is therefore very
important that adequate rests are written into any part, not only to allow
the player to recover breath but also to give time for the muscles to
relax.

The oboe does not compare with the flute for agility of fingering, and
generally speaking oboe parts should not be as 'busy' as those written
for the flute and, to a lesser extent, the clarinet.

Range

The normal working
range for the oboe
is:

For elementary
players, it is
advisable to keep
within:

Do's and don't's

In the examples given below O = no octave key: 1 = 1st octave key

2 = 2nd octave key: D = D key vented

F = forked F fingering, vented

Two tunes, one good, one bad:

Comment: The first exploits the attacking quality of oboe articulation,
lies well under the fingers, and is within the best range. The second
involves not only wide slurred leaps, but also a series of awkward fingerings. Oboe mechanisms are various and, generally speaking, 'student'
models lack the extra keys which facilitate certain progressions. The
most important of these is the 'F vent'. Unlike the Boehm system flute
and clarinet, the oboe has to 'fork' finger F before or after any note
requiring RH 3 on the D key. In this case, the note must be vented and
unless an automatic 'F vent' is fitted, the E^b key must do duty. This is
a long stretch for some young hands and additionally complicates certain
finger patterns.

The oboe overblows at the octave and effectively requires three separate
vents to assist the production of the second harmonic. The first of these
is a small hole in the upper D key, and on most cheap instruments LH 1 has
to slide off the hole while keeping down the key. On better instruments
the D key is kept down automatically and the finger can be lifted off. As
this vent is used for c#'', d'' and e^b'', the following progressions if
rapid and slurred,are particularly awkward on 'student' instruments:

It will be seen, therefore, that the second tune above has its problems,
and on a 'student' oboe with single octave keys, the beginner will find it
difficult to hold the pitch steady above a'', where the second octave key
must be applied. As the flute is in any case more effective in this range,
the young oboist should not be asked to play these notes if at all possible.

Wide leaps, with the exception of octaves, should be treated with caution,
particularly when slurred downwards.

Remember that the lowest notes on the oboe are perforce loud. If this
instrument is acting as a lower part to a quiet melody on, say, the flute,
it will almost certainly obscure the upper voice.

Above all, give the player short phrases and plenty of rests.

Tuning: The lowest notes on the oboe are stable. As the column of air is
shortened up to the c'' hole, intonation comes more under the influence of
the reed and there is an increasing tendency to play sharp. From c#'' upwards, stability is once again restored until the second octave key comes
into operation, and from a'' upwards good tuning usually takes time to
achieve.

CLARINET

Characteristics

Among the woodwind and brass normally found in the orchestra, the clarinet
is the only instrument which behaves, acoustically speaking, as a stopped
pipe. Effectively this means that only the odd-numbered harmonics are
present in any strength in its tonal spectrum, and that overblowing produces the twelfth rather than the octave, as is the case with other instruments: [o overblown note / fundamental note]   The result of this is that tonally the
clarinet has three effective registers,
each with its own tone colour. The
lowest, called the chalumeau register, is rich and though quite individual
in quality, blends well with bassoon and horn tone, a fact worth remembering when scoring for a group or small orchestra. The throat notes are by
comparison thin, colourless, and difficult to play in tune. The upper, or
clarino register, is bright and permits expressive even tone. See below
for further comment.

Here is an example of good clarinet writing, from the beginning of the
Trio in Mozart's Symphony no 39 (K 453):

<u>Comment</u>: The two best registers are used and the writing demonstrates the
clarinet in two typical roles: as a melody instrument and as an accompaniment playing broken chords - the one legato and the other staccato.
Generally speaking, the clarinet is the most versatile of the woodwind. It
has a very extensive range, is capable of wide dynamic contrasts, and is
effective in legato and staccato music, as the given example shows. Above
all, it is very flexible in its expressive qualities. It is also agile,
and provided one avoids certain progressions (see below), trills and
tremolo passages are easy and effective. Attack and articulation can be
varied from hard dry tonguing to a soft liquid start to the note. In view
of all this, it is not surprising that in a wind band the clarinet takes
the same important role as the violin in an orchestra, since both instruments have the quality of expressive flexibility.

To sum up, the clarinet can be used as a solo instrument, as the bass to
upper wind, and to fill in the harmony; it is particularly suited to middle
parts in quiet music.

<u>Breathing</u>

Since it requires neither as much breath as the flute nor as little as the
oboe, the clarinet poses no real problems for the young player in this respect. The sustained pressure associated with the double-reed instruments
is not a feature of the single-reed clarinet.

<u>Range</u>

The clarinet is a transposing instrument (see pp 150-3); the standard model
is built in B♭. All references here are to 'written' notes, sounding a
tone lower: 'written' C sounds 'concert' B♭.
The normal working range for the clarinet is:

The instrument will play much higher, but for
present purposes, c''' should be taken as the
upper limit. Beyond this, control of tuning and dynamics becomes more
difficult, and the tone is loud and penetrating in quality. It is important
to realize not only the tonal differences between the three registers and
the difficulty in obtaining even and gradual matching of timbre in moving
from one to another, but also the implications in fingering the instrument.
As already mentioned (p 37), the standard fingering LH 1-2-3 : RH 1-2-3-4
produces f in the chalumeau register, while the overblowing, encouraged by
the speaker key, produces c'' in the clarino register.

The basic fingering for the scales on
these two notes is the same, apart
from the addition of the speaker key:

The notes f' to b♭' have to be played by opening
small holes at the top of the clarinet, while b♮'
is the harmonic of the lowest note on the instrument, e:

It will be seen that b♭' is played with the whole tube opened and b♮' with
whole tube closed, apart from the speaker key. The so-called 'break' is
therefore strictly between b♭' (or a♯') and b♮', and this and other progressions from throat notes to the lower end of the clarino register
should be treated with an awareness for the fingering problems involved,
especially in rapid slurred passages such as:

These will be almost impossible for all but expert players. Beginners
usually start by playing chalumeau notes. For effective results with the
inexpert player, keep within this range and up to about g'' in the clarino
register, treating progressions across the throat and clarino registers
with caution.

Do's and don't's

The main fingering problems have already been discussed. When writing
tremolos or arpeggio passages, at which the clarinet is peculiarly adept,
avoid too wide intervals, especially with high notes, where a third should
be the maximum. In the chalumeau register, a fifth or sixth is possible.
Unlike other woodwind, the clarinet, overblowing at the twelfth rather
than at the octave, can find octave leaps awkward.

Case Study 6:   Act 2 Finale from The Magic Flute by Mozart

Originally for pairs of clarinets and bassoons, this arrangement for a
quartet of clarinets demonstrates good writing for the clarinet in its
best ranges. There is also scope for really musical phrasing, soft and
hard tonguing (the latter at the _fp_ in bar 8), staccato and legato playing,
and wide dynamic contrasts. Notice that only the second clarinet has to
play 'across the break'. Concert pitch is as in the original:

Act 2 : Finale : The Magic Flute : Mozart

Notice that each part has a separate stave. This makes it easier to write
in phrase and dynamic markings and avoids the problem, especially associated with clarinet writing, of notes and beams standing clear either side
of an empty stave, as they would in the last three bars of the quartet if
it was reduced to a duo:

Tuning: Apart from the throat notes, which are as difficult to play in
tune as to finger, a reasonably well-made instrument should provide few
problems as regards intonation.

BASSOON

Characteristics

The bassoon, like the oboe, is a conical double-reed instrument, and while
it shares many of the characteristics and problems of the smaller instrument, it has a number of both which are peculiarly its own. Like the oboe,
it has a somewhat biting tone, varying from rich and resonant notes in the
lowest register — using what is in effect the extension provided by the
doubled-back bore — to a gradual refining of tone as one moves up through
the basic scale of F to the top of the overblown octave ending at f'. The
top register, which even in Mozart's time extended to b♭', three octaves
above the bottom note, tends to sound more strained and pinched, and inexperienced players may have difficulty in controlling the pitch and timbre
of the highest notes.

The characteristic tone of the bassoon, at its best in the middle octave
B♭ to b♭, is partially conditioned by the extended finger holes in the
wing joint, which act as subsidiary resonators, and by the quality of the
reed. No two instruments are alike, even if one ignores the basic differences between the German (Heckel) and the French (Buffet) models, the
latter of which is becoming obsolete and is certainly almost never seen in
professional hands outside its mother country. Variations in fingering
are common, particularly for high notes.

Articulation, though not as bright as with the oboe, is a feature of the
bassoon. The lowest notes require time to speak, especially in soft
passages, but generally the bassoon can supply a staccato bass line which,
if coupled with cello and/or double bass, will add considerable weight,
clarity, and attack. In the first example, from the 'Haffner' Symphony
(K 385) by Mozart, bassoons join bowed lower strings, while in the second,
the beginning of the slow movement of Haydn's 'Clock' Symphony, pizzicato
violins, cellos and basses are doubled by staccato bassoons, playing here
in thirds:

The bassoon plays other roles within the orchestra or ensemble. A study
of Haydn's writing for the instrument is rewarding. It can fill in the
harmony; it blends especially well with clarinets and horns in its tenor
range. It also serves effectively as a solo instrument. The following
example well illustrates the singing baritone range of the bassoon:

The bassoon is the only woodwind instrument not to use the treble clef.
The bass clef is standard, while for extended passages in the upper register, the tenor clef ╪ is adopted, as with the orchestral trombone and
cello.

Breathing and fatigue: much the same applies as with the oboe, though not
to the same extent. For youngsters, the bassoon is tiring to hold as well
as to blow, and rests must be written into a part. Though rapid tonguing
is possible and effective, avoid lengthy staccato passage work, which is
fatiguing.

Range

The normal working range for the bassoon is:

For elementary players, it is advisable to keep within the
following range, with occasional notes above and below:

Outside F to d, fingerings do not repeat, although the bassoon overblows
at the octave. Even within the given ranges, the tenor notes g to c need
a mixture of half-holing and the LH thumb operating either the crook key or
one of two other vents. If c♯ is included in a passage, this involves yet
another key for the LH thumb (see below).

Do's and don't's

The potential versatility of the bassoon is often underestimated. It has
a wide range and is capable of very expressive playing in its tenor range,
in both legato and staccato music. Apart from its obvious function as a
bass line instrument, it can be used to fill in the harmony, blending well
with other woodwind and horns, and it can also reinforce a soprano melody
by doubling it at the lower octave.

However, it does have fingering problems, as already mentioned. In the
following example the player of a German type of bassoon needs a very active LH thumb:

a = half-hole LH 1   c = vent A key on   <u>note</u>: b - d all involve
b = crook key on   d = vent C key on   LH thumb

This extract from Mozart's 'Jupiter' Symphony would be much easier to play
on the now obsolete French type of bassoon.
The lowest notes from $B^b{}'$ to E^b are difficult to attack quietly and require
the LH thumb to move across another three keys. It is therefore impossible
to play with any rapidity, especially slurred notes. Avoid all scalic
passages below the bass stave for elementary players. The following, however, is quite possible:

Avoid wide downward slurs. Even the following, from <u>The Magic Flute</u>, will
pose problems at * :

<u>Trills and tremolos</u>: one finger trills are easy and effective, but others
can be impossible. Discussion with a player is the quickest way of finding
out what is viable.
Remember that the 'break' occurs between f and f$^\sharp$. Avoid rapid slurred
passages such as the following:

<u>Tuning</u>: given a good instrument and reed, as well as an aurally sensitive
player who has learnt to 'lip' or to find alternative fingerings for poor
notes, all should be well. But this is taking a lot for granted!

SAXOPHONE

Characteristics

Although made of metal, the saxophone is classified as a woodwind instrument. It has a single reed and a conical bore. Alto, tenor, and baritone
are the most likely to be found in general use. Their tone is familiar
from their wide association with dance, jazz, and show bands. When played
without vibrato they can blend well with brass and lower woodwind, for
whose absent members they often deputize in school and youth orchestras.
They also have a legitimate place in concert wind and military bands and,
like Renaissance consorts of family instruments, saxophone quartets exist
in their own right.

The saxophone is as flexible and agile as the clarinet, though rapid articulation, especially with the larger members of the family, is not easy to
achieve. With a mouthpiece and reed similar to that of the clarinet, the
saxophone is easy to 'blow' and, since it overblows at the octave, the
fingering resembles that of the oboe. The standard scale (LH 1-2-3 RH 1-2-3-4)
for all saxophones is C major. Being trans-
posing instruments, they sound concert:
Parts are written in the treble clef.

Range

The normal written range for all instruments is:

The sounding equivalents are:
A few higher notes are possible
for experienced players.

From this it will be seen that saxophones can substitute for the following
instruments which have generally similar ranges:

    Alto saxophone in E$^\flat$:   B$^\flat$ clarinet, B$^\flat$ trumpet, E$^\flat$ tenor horn*

    Tenor saxophone in B$^\flat$:   B$^\flat$ euphonium*, B$^\flat$ tenor trombone*, bassoon

    Baritone saxophone in E$^\flat$: B$^\flat$ tenor trombone, E$^\flat$ bass*, bassoon

    *no further transposition required, unless the trombone is written in
    the bass clef.

Note: if an E$^\flat$ treble clef transposing instrument such as baritone saxophone or E$^\flat$ bass has to read off a bass clef part, read
as for treble clef and add three sharps or remove three
flats from the key signature:

Do's and don't's

There's little to add. The 'break', all fingers off to all fingers on,
occurs between c#' and d', and one should avoid rapid slurred passages
between these notes and those immediately above and below.

Arranging for woodwind

While the tradition of writing for wind goes back to the Renaissance, the
full development of the orchestral instruments dates only from about 1750.
Then, horns were generally added to oboes, clarinets and bassoons in
ensemble music, as in the Serenades and Divertimenti of Haydn and Mozart
(see pp 58-9). The standard wind quintet of one each of woodwind and a horn
was established in the quintets of Danzi and Reicha, contemporaries of
Beethoven. However, it is only in recent years that easy woodwind ensemble
music has been written to satisfy the growing needs of young players, and
it is with this type of repertoire that we are concerned. It is assumed
that the detailed information given on pp 36-49 has been absorbed.

The woodwind family

Only the flute, oboe, clarinet, and bassoon will be considered. It is of
course possible to write music for an ensemble of one type of instrument,
and the popularity of the transverse flute in the early eighteenth century
is reflected in the many duets and trios by Boismortier, Telemann, and
others. More recently an extensive repertoire of music for clarinets has
appeared (see pp 44-5). Flutes and clarinets blend well together, as do
the two double-reed instruments, but generally the woodwind are contrasted
in tone colour, unlike the homogeneous string and brass families.

We are here concerned with the problems which arise in writing and arranging music for the four different instruments playing as a group, problems
which exist equally for the woodwind within the wind band and orchestra.
In view of the large number of clarinettists, the addition of a second
part for this instrument will not only help to employ available talent but,
assuming five players to four parts, will allow staggered rests in all
parts. The problem of fatigue in young wind players is a real one.

Part-writing

Flute, oboe, and clarinet are all soprano instruments and all can therefore
take the top part in standard four-part writing. However, the following
points must be kept firmly in mind. The flute is weak in its lowest register, gaining strength and penetration as it goes higher. The oboe is the
opposite, strong in the lowest octave and becoming thinner through its
second register. It is therefore quite ineffective to score a hymn tune
from a short score with the flute on the melody and the oboe on the alto
part. The tune will be inaudible. Putting the flute up an octave will
create too large a gap between the melody and the accompanying harmony —
rather as if a small boy was to wear a bow tie around his bare neck, with
nothing else on but a pair of shorts, socks and shoes.

Care must also be taken to avoid giving the clarinet important melodic material 'across the break', for not only may the fingering be awkward, but tone and tuning will almost certainly be poor. The lower register of the clarinet makes an effective tenor voice, while the bassoon, apart from its main function as a bass instrument, can also contribute a middle part while the clarinet plays the bass line.

Case Study 7 (p 52) is concerned with the basic distribution and range of parts in a simple four-part song.

Dynamics
Dynamic markings in woodwind music have to be carefully considered, taking into account the relative tonal power of each instrument in any of its registers. Experienced players accommodate themselves to 'blanket' markings, automatically adjusting to a dynamic level which will retain the correct balance. For the inexperienced, detailed individual marking is advised as an aid to achieving the desired musical performance. An obvious example: mark up low-lying flutes, mark down low-lying oboes. Breath marks (✓) should be inserted where helpful and not obvious (as in a rest).

Suitable keys
Flat keys are better than sharp keys: see p 37.

The score
Regardless of which instrument is playing the 'lead', the normal order from top to bottom is flute, oboe, clarinet (if two, then on separate staves: see p 45), bassoon.

CASE STUDIES
Each study illustrates a standard type of arrangement. The first, a transcription, has already been mentioned. The second is an example of translation from brass to woodwind, while the third reduces a six-part Mozart score to woodwind quartet.

Case Study 7:   Song no 46 by Orlando Gibbons

This piece has already appeared as Case Study 1, where it was transcribed
for brass quartet. There, problems of balance between the trumpet melody
and accompanying harmony did not arise, since the top instrument was quite
well able to hold its own against the others. The problems in arranging
it successfully for woodwind are much greater, as the following analysis
will show.

The original short score is as follows:

A straight transcription in the key of F, with flute on the soprano part,
oboe on the alto, clarinet on the tenor, and bassoon on the bass will not
work. The tune is far too low to be effective, while the alto part goes
below the range of the oboe. Before trying the piece in another key —
less suitable for accompanying community singing — other ways of arranging
the tune should be explored.

If the flute and oboe are put up an octave, too large a gap will open up
between the alto and tenor parts — our little boy has now acquired a shirt
to go with his bow tie, but has lost his pants, even if he still has his
socks and shoes on.

Still keeping the flute on the melody, up an octave, and giving the tenor
part to the oboe, also up an octave, and the alto to the clarinet at its
original pitch, we now have a gap between the bass-line and all other
parts. This layout is quite acceptable. Our little boy now has tie,
shirt and pants, and though he has lost his socks, he still has shoes on,
and is therefore fit to present himself in polite conventional musical
company. Unfortunately the analogy here breaks down, for the musician
will tell you that while it is usually possible to invert the inner parts
without offending traditional harmonic principles, to wear your pants
above your shirt might be considered a little odd.

In the version below, notice that in bar 2 the clarinet has leaped an
octave in order to improve the spacing of parts, and the crotchet D
completes the triad. The clarinet has not been given the original tenor
line, since it lies across the weakest notes on the instrument.

Another version in the original key is now proposed. The clarinet in its
second register blends well with the flute, and while it is not generally
advisable to 'cross parts' in vocal music, there is no valid reason why
this should be the case in instrumental writing. Still faithful to
Gibbons' melody and bass, assigned to flute and bassoon, the arrangement
allows for the oboe and clarinet to interchange, first one and then the
other acting as alto or tenor. Notice how the leap of an octave on a
repeated note in bars 3 and 5 makes this possible.

Transposition of an original piece, especially if in sharp keys, should
always be considered when writing for a wind ensemble which includes the
clarinet. This problem does not arise in the example under discussion,
as F is a very suitable key. However, there may be other considerations,
such as whether the music lies within the best register of a given instrument. Let us explore the possible advantages of transposing this piece
into B flat.

Here again, the flute would be virtually inaudible playing the melody at
the given pitch; the oboe would overpower it on the alto part. By
exchanging these two instruments, the problem would be solved, although
the flute would be confined to an accompanying role in its weakest register. A further possibility would be to keep the tune in the oboe and
write a descant for the flute. In the version below, essentially of the
'faux-bourdon' type, the clarinet is sometimes above and sometimes below
the melody, which must be treated as a solo and therefore marked up so as
not to be obscured.

Case Study 8: Intrada by Johann Pezel

Pezel was a <u>Stadtpfeiffer</u>, or town wait of Leipzig, and this example of
'tower music' — that is, music played from a gallery or the top of a city
building — is found in a collection published in 1685. Originally for
cornetts and sackbuts, this modern edition has been transcribed for B♭
trumpets and three trombones. The redistribution of parts for the woodwind quintet has been added into the score, to make the subsequent arrangement easier to follow.

INTRADA   Johann Pezel (1685)

INTRADA   Johann Pezel (1685)

In making this arrangement for a quintet which includes two clarinets,
care has been taken to ensure that the main melodic lines stand out, not
so much as by marking them up as by placing them in the best registers
of the flute, oboe, and clarinet. The imitation in bars 3 - 5 and 9 - 10
gives all instruments an opportunity to take part in the general discourse.

The piece has been transposed up a fourth into E♭, allowing the flute to
be heard in its more penetrating upper register. At the same time it
enables the clarinet to share in the writing for the original two top
parts without falling foul of the notes in the weakest range of the
instrument.

Only in bars 9 - 12 of Pezel's layout has the sounding order of parts
been altered, where the oboe plays the original fourth part up an octave,
as it would tend to sound too loud in the tenor range, coming on the
lowest notes of the instrument. Alternatively, one could switch oboe
and clarinet 2 parts during these bars. The given distribution is
suggested as preferable since it gives clarinet 2 an interesting passage
in what would otherwise be much the dullest part.

All phrasing and dynamic marks are editorial, both in the published
edition and in the woodwind arrangement.

Case Study 9: Trio from Divertimento no 8 (K 213) by Mozart

Mozart scored the work from which this movement is taken for pairs of
oboes, horns, and bassoons. Like much wind music of its period, its
reduction and translation to smaller and more readily available forces
can be very effective. Study the original and particularly the hand-horn
writing, which makes very effective use of natural harmonics in the
key of F, to which the music modulates from bars 7 - 18.

Trio from Divertimento no 8 (K 213)   Mozart (1775)

What are the problems to be solved in arranging this Trio for woodwind
quartet? At the given pitch, it is obvious that transferring Mozart's
first oboe part to a flute will render it inaudible in many bars, especially if the second oboe part is to remain on an oboe. The first bassoon
part will have to be shared out, and will obviously fit the lower register
of a clarinet. The two horn parts fulfil both a solo role and a 'filler'
function: they must be carefully studied to ensure that where they are
essential they are represented in the arrangement, as in bars 17 - 18,
where the second horn provides the bass-line below the second bassoon.
In the arrangement which follows, look for the answers to the problems
outlined above.

Notice these points:

a) The oboe leads wherever there is a risk of the flute being drowned, as
    in bars 1 - 4, 6 - 10, and 16 - 17.

b) The clarinet not only takes most of the original first bassoon part, as
    at the start of each half, but telescopes both oboe parts in bars 9-12

and takes over oboe 2 in bars 18 to the end, blending well in thirds with the flute.

c) The horn parts have been variously treated, and at the start of the second half, horn 1's duet with bassoon 1 has been transposed up an octave, now shared between flute and clarinet. Apart from bars 17-18, already mentioned, the harmonic function of the horns is essential only in bar 12, where the oboe now plays the major third of the chord.

d) Dynamic markings have been amplified, especially where the flute is in close contention with the oboe, as in bars 7 - 12. Slurs and staccato dots, partially supplied by Mozart, have been regularized, and the editorial phrase markings, as in the quaver passages in bars 7 - 8 and 19-20, should ensure a rhythmic performance.

SUMMARY

The most important factors to consider in making an arrangement for woodwind are:

a) The suitability of the music: see pp 167-9 for source material.

b) The understanding of the tonal contrasts and blends between instruments.

c) Parts written in character and style for each instrument.

d) An awareness of the physical problems of young wind players.

Chapter IV
Brass: The instruments

FAMILY CHARACTERISTICS

The following physical characteristics are common to all so-called 'brass' or lip-reed instruments: a cup-shaped mouthpiece coupled to a tapered tube which ends in a flared bell. With the trombone's slide and the piston and rotary valve, it is obvious that sections of the tube must have parallel walls. However, the resulting stepped bore is acoustically conical, and before the invention of the piston valve early in the nineteenth century, only the notes of the harmonic series could be sounded, their number being determined by the length and width of the bore.

With the adoption of the valve and the development of the tuba family, the brass finally achieved a fully chromatic compass and the ability to play a wide repertoire. Improved performing techniques resulted from the demands made by Wagner in his operas, by the developing military bands and, most importantly for the amateur musician, by the competitive brass band movement. It is essential that those involved in working with junior brass players understand the technicalities of scoring for a wide variety of instruments.

Tone

The tone of modern brass instruments is rounder and stronger than that produced by earlier models. The loss of some of the distinctive quality of the trumpet, horn, and trombone has been partially compensated for by a better blend of timbre within the family as a whole. In the case of the brass band, most of whose instruments either derive from or are very similar to members of the wide-bore Saxhorn family of tubas, the matching of tone can compare with that of a string orchestra or a first-rate choir. The dynamic range of all brass instruments is very wide, and the pianissimo chording of a brass section can be as effective as the full blast of a fortissimo bark.

Attack and legato

The player's lips take the place of the reed in a woodwind instrument, hence the description of the brass family as 'lip-reed' instruments. The tongue acts as a valve, and as with woodwind, it is possible to achieve a hard or soft attack. Legato playing forms an integral part of technique, always remembering that the larger the instrument and the louder the note, the more breath is required to sustain a long phrase. Wide slurred intervals are more difficult to execute than narrow ones. The following example from Richard Strauss's Don Quixote demonstrates some of the problems.

Written originally for tenor tuba, it is playable on a B♭ euphonium, and it
is here written at concert pitch:

It should go without saying that this solo, which though hard for breathing
and legato is quite possible to play well on a valved bass instrument,
would be impossible on the slide trombone, where only adjacent harmonics
sharing the same slide position can be properly slurred. In the quoted
example, the leaps marked * could be nearly slurred, with the slight risk
of interposing the middle harmonics:

Good players learn to slide quickly and the advanced technique of lip and
soft tongue slurring gives the impression of legato playing. Even so, the
Strauss example is clearly not suited to the trombone.

If it takes longer to make a large instrument speak, then the opposite is
true, for the trumpet articulates clearly at speed, and the following
example would be ineffective on any other member of the brass family—
even the trumpet will be pressed to cope with the tonguing at the speed
suggested. Modern music calls for double and triple tonguing on the
smaller instruments, but this is technically advanced playing:

Continuous rapid tonguing is tiring, especially for the lower-pitched instruments, but a brass sforzando or <u>fp</u> attack, either in unison or in
chorus, is very effective - and proportionately more effective the less it
is used.

<u>Suitable music: different genres of brass</u>

Any useful discussion on repertoire presupposes an understanding of orchestral brass, the brass band and the concert wind band.

<u>Orchestral brass</u>: for the purposes of this book, an orchestral brass sec-
tion may consist of as little as one trumpet or the standard small orchestra line-up of two trumpets, one or two horns, and trombone. If the section is to be scored for as an integral group, then an E♭ brass bass will

be a useful addition, since the tenor trombone is not a very effective bass instrument.

In view of the changed role of the horn in the orchestra (see p 156) it is suggested that orchestral scoring practice should follow that of the standard brass ensemble, with trumpets at the top of the score.

The Brass Band: This is dealt with more fully on pp 128-34. Here it is sufficient to say that the Brass Band has a history, repertoire, and tradition of its own. Much encouragement has been given in recent years to leading composers to provide suitably challenging music, and the cloth-cap image is at last being lost. In the Promenade Concert Season of 1974 for the first time two of Britain's best bands played a tough new work by Harrison Birtwistle, which should bury this image for ever. Much of the repertoire of brass bands consists of marches, selections from musical comedy, and competition pieces. It is easy to belittle the quality of such music, but great pleasure, both social and musical, is enjoyed by the brass player who may only add a tonic-dominant 'oompah' to a Sousa march at the weekly rehearsal. It should be appreciated that the rapid progress which can be made by youngsters on brass band instruments with their unified and simple fingering systems outstrips anything that can be matched by strings and woodwind.

The Concert Wind Band: Derived from the military band of woodwind, brass, and percussion, the Concert Wind Band is the outstanding feature of American high school music and it is now rapidly taking root in other countries. Though one may regret the implied lack of able string players to match the abundance of excellent young wind instrumentalists in forming full orchestras, the existence of original and arranged music at advanced performing standards provides a real challenge to test the skills of the large numbers of wind players who would otherwise have to 'double up' or simply fail to get into a full orchestra. One advantage of this type of band is that the lead, taken by clarinets instead of violins, can absorb the large numbers who learn to play this popular and cheap instrument. The published repertoire is still influenced by military considerations, but original works exist, as for example Vaughan Williams's Folk Song Suite and Hindemith's Konzertmusik of 1927. Arrangements of classical and modern music are available and the technical mastery of a first-rate American school band in a work such as one of Richard Strauss's tone poems has to be heard to be believed.

At a more mundane level, much simple music is suitable for arrangement for brass ensemble — hymn tunes, Renaissance dances, and other short pieces. Fatigue can be a problem with young players, and adequate rests must be written into pieces of any length. Exposed entries and long passages at

the top of the range are to be avoided. Overall the range should be restricted to a twelfth, and to as little as an octave for elementary players.
Brass repertoire will be further considered on pp 81 and 167-70.

Suitable keys

Since most brass are transposing instruments in B$^\flat$ and E$^\flat$ (see p 151
for a detailed list), it should be evident that flat keys are the easiest
for group work. A piece of music in E$^\flat$ will have all B$^\flat$ instruments
written in F, E$^\flat$ instruments in C, the F orchestral horn in B$^\flat$, the bass
clef orchestral trombone in E$^\flat$, and the treble clef transposing trombone
in F.

Case Study 10

This may be an unlikely ensemble,
but it is perfectly valid, although on paper the score appears
somewhat odd, with the horn above
the trumpet and the bass line
above everything else. Notice
that the E$^\flat$ treble clef part
looks the same as it sounds in
concert bass clef.
Fingerings are indicated by
figures: see below.

Fingerings

Valves, whether piston or rotary, add sufficient length of extra tubing to
lower any harmonic (or open note = 0) by a tone (first valve = 1), a semitone (second valve = 2), a tone and a half (third valve = 3), or any combination of the three valves, adding up to an augmented 4th.
The fourth valve fitted to some instruments will be discussed at the appropriate points.
The fingering chart which follows covers the written middle range, c' - c''
of all standard brass instruments, based on the 2nd, 3rd, and 4th harmonics,
shown in all charts as white notes. These are common to all but the horn
in F, whose extra length provides the 4th to 8th harmonics at this pitch
and whose fingerings are given above. Below the standard fingerings are
the slide positions, numbered 1 - 7, of the transposing B$^\flat$ trombone,
which sounds down a ninth:

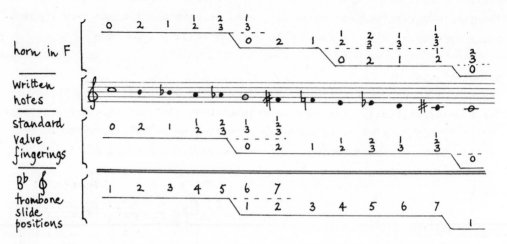

Preferred fingerings are those immediately above the solid line. Where
there are alternative fingerings, as for G and F♯ in the chart above,
players will generally use those involving fewest valves. In the case of
the trombone, the nearest position will be chosen:

It must be emphasized that the scale above gives the <u>written</u> notes. If for
example, the E♭ tenor horn reads the given notes, they will sound down a
major sixth, giving a chromatic scale from e♭' to e♭.

Extending the fingering chart above and below the written C scale, the range
c' down to g and g'' down to c'' represents the advised limits, with the
proviso that wide-bore instruments such as the euphonium in B♭ encourage
easy production of low notes, while the narrow-bore trumpet facilitates the
upper end of the range. It will be seen that at the top end of the range
the choice of fingerings is wide:

Special effects: Muting

Mutes can be used on all brass instruments, modifying the timbre to a
slightly nasal sound and facilitating very quiet playing. Muted brass
played loudly produce a hard tone. Allow plenty of time for placing the
mute in the bell (<u>con sord</u>), and for removing it (<u>ord</u>).
While many different types of mute can be had reasonably cheaply for the
trumpet and cornet, this is not the case with larger instruments. Before
specifying mutes, make sure that they are available. They probably won't
be for the tuba.

Problems with hand-stopping the horn are discussed on p 69.

Trills

On most brass instruments, trills can be played on the lips provided that
the harmonics are sufficiently close. These are similar to vocal trills,
but they are too difficult for the average player and should therefore be
avoided.
Valves can also be used to produce trills, but they tend to be sluggish on
the larger instruments. A trill which involves the use of all three
valves will not be very effective, as for instance the following:

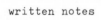 

written notes

On the whole, avoid trills on the trombone and the bass brass instruments.

THE INSTRUMENTS

These are listed in descending order of pitch. Those marked with an
asterisk are associated essentially with brass bands. General points
already discussed will not be repeated.
TRUMPET
As with the horn and trombone, trumpets were formerly crooked in different
keys. The standard instrument today is pitched in B$\flat$, though the C
trumpet is finding increased favour. Small trumpets in D and F are used
for high clarino parts in Baroque music. However, for present purposes,
only the B$\flat$ instrument will be considered, and all examples will be

transposed accordingly, whatever the original specification may have been.

Characteristics

As the soprano instrument of the brass family, the trumpet's bright and
incisive tone can dominate not only its own section but the orchestra as
a whole. Apart from its traditional function as a 'call to arms', it has
a flexibility of tone and attack which allows it to be treated melodically
much in the manner of an alto woodwind instrument. The examples below
demonstrate these two characteristics:

Orchestrally the trumpet can add its weight to any climactic passage and
is especially effective in a chordal role, not only to reinforce cadential
points but also in quiet held notes which tie the harmony together. The
clarino parts of Bach and his contemporaries are not for the timid and
weak, since they require a high-note technique beyond the range of most
players.

Range

The notes from g to c' are rather weak and of poor quality. Avoid them
for solo work, even if they serve adequately for a second or inside part.
Intonation on these low notes may need correcting by adjustment of the
third valve slide.

CORNET

Characteristics

Though shorter in length and wider in bore, the B♭ cornet has the same
range as the trumpet; its tone is rounder and more mellow. It is

the principal melodic instrument of the brass band, either solo or tutti,
taking the place of the violins in the orchestra. Very flexible in its
middle range, the cornet retains something of the trumpet's brilliance at
the upper end.

The soprano E♭ cornet, concert up a minor third, can take over the highest
phrases from the B♭ cornet, but this instrument is unlikely to be found
outside the full brass band.

The flugelhorn in B♭, really a member of the horn family but looking and
sounding much like a cornet, is used in the full brass band mainly to
double the repiano or tutti cornet.

Most B♭ trumpets and cornets can be converted into instruments pitched in
A by pulling out the main tuning slide and correspondingly lengthening
the valve slides. .Parts written in A can facilitate fingering in the
sharp keys favoured by elementary string players.

HORN

The orchestral horn in F must be differentiated from the brass band E♭
tenor horn, to be discussed later. The F horn is almost twice the length
of the E♭ horn, and its lower fundamental provides a greater number of
open harmonic notes in the middle register. In the following example
showing the written harmonics, notes marked * are not strictly in tune,
while those inside a square ◼ are the harmonics of the E♭ horn.
Concert pitch is down a fifth for the F horn, and down a major sixth for
the E♭ horn.

F horn
written
harmonics

The modern orchestral horn has developed from the coiled hunting horn, on
which only the notes of the harmonic series could be sounded, as shown
above. Those notes within ⌊_____⌋ are difficult except for the best players.

Up to the first years of the nineteenth century the valveless 'natural'
hand horn was the standard instrument, as played in Mozart's concertos.
The addition of long crooks which lowered the fundamental to E♭ or D,
allowed a good player to reach the 16th harmonic, giving a complete scale
at the top. A technique of lipping and hand-stopping went some way
towards correcting faulty notes; this is still done for fine tuning on
the modern instrument. With the invention of the valve players gradually
compromised on an instrument crooked in F, and today most performers use

a wide-bore German-style double horn on which a fourth valve, operated by
the thumb, enables one to switch from a horn in F to one crooked in B♭
above. This shorter B♭ instrument has the advantage of greater stability,
since only the first twelve harmonics are used to reach the same concert
note as will sound from the 16th harmonic on the F horn.

The valve horn, being fully chromatic, dispenses with the need for extra
crooks, and players learn to transpose at sight the old hand horn parts.
Convention now dictates a part written for horn in F. If the player
decides to take it on the B♭ side of his horn, he will do his own transposing.

For all practical purposes, horn parts should be written in the treble
clef, a fifth above the concert note.

Characteristics

Musically speaking, the orchestral horn can justifiably be called the king
of the brass family. Its overall range, its tonal and dynamic flexibility,
and its expressive capability have inspired composers from Mozart and
Brahms to many contemporary writers. Its smooth warm tone blends well
with other instruments. The horn straddles the musical gap between the
woodwind and brass sections in the symphony orchestra. It is widely used
as a melodic soloist, as in the opening bars of Schubert's Symphony no 7,
the 'Great C Major'.

Notice that accidentals are written in as they occur, rather than being
placed in the key signature.

This convention is still
followed as far as horns
are concerned:

Here all four horns in unison introduce the final movement of Bartok's
Concerto with full force and grandeur.

Horn players generally favour either high parts or low parts. When writing
in two parts, these should be treated as soprano and tenor. In a score
requiring four horns, the normal layout is:

Pair 1 { 1 S
         2 T)   Horns 1 and 3 are therefore high
                          note players, and 2 and 4 are low
Pair 2 { 3 A)   note players.
         4 B

Used in pairs, the following type of writing is traditional and still very
effective, if basic, in tonic - dominant - tonic progressions:

Written for hand horns, all notes are harmonics, but the valve instrument
allows this sort of writing to be transposed into any key.

Range

The lowest written harmonics of the horn are theoretical rather than
practical, though on the short B$\flat$ side of the instrument a quiet sustained
pedal concert B$\flat$ below the bass clef can be achieved. On the whole, it is
best to keep within the following written limits:

horn in F
written  = concert

The best range for elementary players lies between written

Special techniques

Stopped notes and muting. Partial insertion of the hand into the bell will
flatten a note by up to a semitone, a technique required to play the hand
horn solo quoted from Schubert's Symphony no 7, if played on a horn in C
basso. This veils the tone, but does not completely mute the horn. However, when the hand is inserted to close the bell completely, this has the
effect of raising the pitch by about a semitone, which has to be compensated for by the player transposing the note or passage down by the same
amount and adjusting the embouchure. This form of muting is indicated by
the words 'stopped' or 'mute' and is cancelled by 'open'. A single muted
note is marked above with +, cancelled by O.

A proper horn mute does not alter the pitch. Before demanding muted playing, ensure that your player either possesses a mute or knows what hand-
stopping means.

The tone of a muted horn tends to be slightly edgy and metallic.

Brassy (cuivré). This effect results from hard blowing and increased lip
tension. 'Brassy' well describes the sound. The technique can be combined
with stopped notes and is particularly effective on individual notes marked
'stopped' with sfz or ff attack. The resulting tone is biting and snarl-
ing in quality.

*TENOR E$\flat$ HORN

Used in brass bands mainly for accompanying purposes, the tenor horn has a
range very similar to the orchestral horn in F. With a lighter tone
quality than the baritone and euphonium, it can also be used for alto

melodic work, either as soloist or tutti with the standard complement of
three horns playing in unison.

TROMBONE

The tenor trombone, pitched in B^b, is the standard orchestral and band
instrument. It is sometimes fitted with a rotary valve or 'plug' operated
by the left thumb which extends the tube to convert it into a bass trombone
in F. This tenor-bass instrument is now in fairly general use, but before
writing below the range of the tenor trombone, ensure that the more complex
instrument is available. For present purposes, only the tenor trombone
will be considered.

Characteristics

The trombone's tone is uniform throughout its range, tending towards brightness at the top end. The lower notes are rather weak and it is a mistake
to use these to provide a firm bass-line, for which other brass instruments,
such as the euphonium and E^b bass, are more suited. Played loudly, the
trombone has great power, as in Schubert's Symphony no 7. Here the trombone
dominates the unison strings which share the theme:

Trombones are also very effective
in quiet music, as in the introduction to the aria 'O Isis and
Osiris' from Mozart's The Magic
Flute:

Notice the legato slurs, which it may or may not be possible to interpret
literally!

Both examples call for three instruments. The inclusion of a bass trombone
was normal in the orchestral section until Wagner inflated it by the addition of tubas of many kinds. At a junior level, the trombone will combine
well with two trumpets and an E^b bass to form a balanced quartet.

In solo writing consideration must be given to the technical problems inherent in playing the instrument. Some of these have already been mentioned
and a study of the slide position charts on pp 63-4 will show that there is,
taking an extreme example, no alternative to moving from 1st to 7th position in the following progressions:

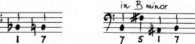

At an elementary level, avoid rapid playing which involves many position changes. This is inevitable at the lower end of the instrument. It is better to write slow-moving melodies in the middle and upper end of the trombone's range, as in the example from Stravinsky's <u>Pulcinella</u> Suite. Slide positions have been added to show the incidence and extent of changes. Any notes under a slur which do not come on the same harmonic or adjacent slide positions will be soft-tongued or lip-slurred, techniques beyond the elementary player:

Range

The orchestral trombone uses the bass and tenor clefs. The alto clef has become obsolete. It is NOT a transposing instrument. When scoring for trombones in the brass band they become transposing instruments in B and parts are written in the treble clef:

Brass band players should have no difficulty in reading the tenor clef, the notes <u>appearing</u> the same on the stave:

Two flats must be subtracted from or two sharps added to the key signature. The lowest notes (E - G), played in extended slide positions, are gener- ally of poor quality and should be avoided if at all possible.

Orchestral bass clef slide position chart

Within the suggested maximum range, which can be extended upwards by skilled players, each position gives the following harmonics:

The seventh harmonic has been omitted from the above chart. This is flat in pitch, but adjusted on the slide the shortened positions (s) will pro- duce the following notes within the suggested ranges given above:

A study of the charts will show that d' can be played in first, fourth and seventh (shortened) positions. Take this into consideration when writing an exposed solo for the trombone.

Special effects: glissando

The glissando is characteristic of the trombone as of no other wind instrument. It can only be effected between a maximum of the seven positions on any one harmonic, a distance of an augmented fourth. Don't overdo it!

*BARITONE AND *EUPHONIUM

Both instruments are pitched in B$\flat$ and like the treble clef trombone, they sound down a ninth from the written treble clef note. As they share many of the same characteristics, they will be considered together.

Characteristics

The baritone's narrower bore makes it suitable for tenor range melodic work and particularly for providing harmonic support to the middle areas of a brass band score. The euphonium is usually considered as a bass-line instrument and, when fitted with a fourth valve, is particularly suited to this role. However, the euphonium's superior tone quality has made it the principal tenor solo instrument in the brass band, to which it relates as the cello does to the orchestra of Dvořák and Tchaikovsky. It has a rich warm tone, a good working range, and is very flexible in execution. It is the smallest of the military tubas, and if it is played orchestrally as a tenor tuba — an example from Strauss's <u>Don Quixote</u> has already been quoted on p 61 — it is written at concert pitch in the bass clef, as with the orchestral trombone. These two instruments are of similar length, but the euphonium's wider bore encourages a better tone at the lower end of its range.

Range

B$\flat$ baritone and euphonium: written = concert

The baritone has a marginally lighter tone and is easier to play at the top end of the range.

*E$\flat$ BRASS BASS

Characteristics

This military tuba, adopted by the brass band and generally known as the E$\flat$ bass, is commonly found in youth orchestras doing duty for the true orchestral tuba. If fitted with a descending fourth valve, the downward range can be extended chromatically to the fundamental, concert E$\flat$'. The range given below relates to the three-valve bass. Orchestral tuba parts

are written at concert pitch in the bass clef, while brass band convention
demands tranposed parts in the treble clef. A bass player should therefore
be familiar with both notational systems. The wide bore of the instrument
encourages facility on the lower notes, though the tonal range is even,
with wide dynamic possibilities over two octaves. The E♭ bass is almost
the equal of the cornet in coping with rapid passage work.

Range   E♭ 𝄞 bass: written ♪♪♪♪   sounding as 𝄢 ♪♪♪
                                              orchestral tuba

*BB♭ BRASS BASS

Characteristics

The brass equivalent of the string double bass, the BB♭ bass usually
doubles the E♭ bass at the lower octave. It almost never has a fourth
valve. The tone is somewhat ponderous, and it is seldom found in junior
ensembles, but is a regular member of the full brass band.[1]

Range   BB♭ bass: written ♪♪♪♪   = concert 𝄢 ♪♪♪

SUMMARY: Do's and don't's

All other things being equal, choose the instrument with the best natural
range for a given part, rather than writing at the extreme ends of the tessitura. Tone quality must of course be considered, but remember that 'the
art of the possible' should be the first consideration when dealing with
the inexperienced player.

Lip and breath fatigue will soon overcome the best of intentions in a long
high passage. The odd top note will not cause much bother, but don't stay
up there. Remember to give adequate rests to allow for recuperation — the
smaller the instrument, the greater the wind pressure: the longer and
larger the bore, the greater the volume of air required to make it speak.
Either way, playing a brass instrument is hard physical work. Always consider the effort required of the young player, and avoid long tied notes
played fortissimo.

Exposed high entries are risky. A cue, transposed as appropriate, may pre-
vent a falsely pitched entry.

Having sounded warnings, it would be wrong to underestimate the ability of
the young. Many brass instruments are easy to play up to a reasonable
standard, and progress is more rapid than with strings and woodwind. In
writing for mixed groups, the brass can be stretched to a higher degree of
competence than that possible for other families of instruments.

[1]Those interested in the complexities of the tuba family and its history
are referred to: Cecil Forsyth, Orchestration (London, 1948), pp 151-63.

Arranging for brass

GENERAL PRINCIPLES

This section is concerned with the brass ensemble, not the brass band (see
p 128). Much has already been said on p 63 about suitable keys, and the
fingering and optimum ranges of individual instruments. Here we are concerned with making a satisfactory compromise in writing for an imposed or
selected group.

The brass family

Ignoring duo and trio combinations, the following ensembles are commonly
found: 4-part   5-part

	4-part		5-part
S	trumpet/cornet	S	trumpet/cornet
A	trumpet/cornet	A	trumpet/cornet
T	horn in F/trombone	A/T	horn in F or E$^\flat$ trombone/baritone
B	trombone/E$^\flat$ bass	T/Bar	trombone/euphonium
		B	E$^\flat$ bass/ tenor-bass trombone

Compared with strings and woodwind, the overall compass of a brass ensemble
is restricted, a point to be kept in mind when selecting material for
arrangement.

It is always possible to double up parts in a group, especially the top and
bottom lines. However, rather than risk both players tiring at the same
time, it may be advisable to alternate, each taking a phrase and only doubling up in tutti or loud passages.

Part-writing

The normal layout by voice designation is as suggested above. If a baritone
or euphonium is available, try to use it as a solo instrument; its written
range is as for the trumpet or cornet, though sounding down an octave, and
it can therefore play similar melodic material, providing relief from the
rather insistent tone of the smaller instruments. Remember that any solo
for the trombone must take account of the instrument's limitations as
regards agility and legato phrasing, qualities more associated with the
euphonium.

At a very elementary level, keep phrases short. Breath marks should be inserted where necessary and all parts must be marked with dynamics. A correct balance between voices can only be achieved in rehearsal, especially
in a general loud or quiet passage, but if one instrument is to stand out,
then mark the parts accordingly.

In the Case Studies, parts have been numbered (1), (2), (3) etc. to facilitate reference to the original and/or arrangement in the subsequent analysis.

The score

There are many different ways of writing out a brass score. Does one write
at concert pitch, with transposed individual parts? Or should the score

show only the written notes? This may be easier in discussing points at
rehearsal but can be difficult to read, musically speaking, as was demons-
trated on p 63 with the hymn tune 'Austria'.

There is no firm tradition, and one can only suggest adopting the most practical method for any given piece or ensemble, as in the Case Studies which
follow.

CASE STUDIES

These have been chosen to demonstrate different types of treatment, arising
from the musical character of each piece. The first, very short and there-
for suitable for beginners, may be taken as being typical of the harmonic
genre found widely in Renaissance dance music. With the exceptions noted
below, this is a straight transcription.

Case Study 11:'Branle Simple': Second livre de danseries: Pierre Attaingnant

Pitch: The arrangement is at the original pitch.

Range: A feature of much music of the period intended for recorders, crumhorns, and other instruments whose compass was only about a tenth, is the narrow range of each part. This suits elementary brass players, and here the music lies comfortably within the middle range of the designated instruments.

Breathing: There are obvious breathing points at the end of each set of three bars. Intermediate breath marks have been inserted. These may be necessary, depending on tempo and volume.

Alterations to the original: Only two have been made, apart from editorial accidentals.

a)   bar 2: ④ had:

In order to avoid the awkward leap of a seventh, the low G has been put up an octave.

b)   bar 8: ① had:

Rather than leap up a seventh after the quaver D, the scale has been run down to C, with an octave leap, an easy interval for brass beginners. For better players, the original should be quite possible.

Dynamics: The original has no markings. A possible scheme would be:

A:A // B:B // A:A

f/p // f/p // p/f

One could also alter the instrumentation (see below), or, if there is more than one player to a part, the piano sections might be played by a solo quartet.

Alternative instruments

a)   ① and ② :   cornets

b)   ② :   horn in F

c)   ③ :   trombone, baritone or euphonium

d)   ④ :   euphonium or E♭ bass

Any of the above suggestions would not alter the concert pitch of the voices. However, it would be quite effective to arrange the whole piece, or a repeated section, as follows:

① :   baritone
② :   euphonium } as written, but sounding down an octave

③ :   trombone or euphonium - re-written to sound down an octave

④ :   E♭ bass - a newly written part, which has been added under the given arrangement, taking as much as possible down an octave.

This would take the whole piece down an octave. Assuming a baritone or euphonium on ③, it would also be in order to interchange parts ① and ③, putting the trumpet on ③ and the lower instrument on ①. In music of this kind, the melody can sound as well on a middle voice.

Case Study 12: <u>Theme from the Largo of Symphony no 9 'From the New World'</u>
                                                            <u>by Dvořák</u>

This famous cor anglais solo, joined by clarinet and bassoon and accompanied by muted strings, makes a very suitable piece for brass band instruments. The lower parts move slowly, while the melody can be conveniently
shared between tenor horn and cornets. This is an example of translation
and reduction.

Arrangement for brass band ensemble

Pitch: The downward transposition into B♭ from the original D♭ simplifies
the fingering for all instruments.

Range: All parts, sounding in concert B♭, lie comfortably within the range
of the suggested instruments. Notice that the featured horn and cornets
have very simple parts between their solos, giving them a chance to gather
strength for the more important bars.

Breathing: The music divides cleanly into two-bar phrases, and breath marks
have been inserted accordingly.

Alterations to the original: A comparison of Dvořák's score with the arrangement will reveal a reorganization of the inner parts. The original scoring
calls for as many as nine parts, allowing for the divisi strings. The

arrangement is necessarily restricted to six parts, and doublings have
therefore been reduced. The need to keep accompanying parts quiet until
the general crescendo in the last two bars has meant placing the chords in
the lower register of each instrument. At the end, notice how the middle
voices not only rise in pitch, but are more active in movement. This all
helps to create increased tension which is relaxed in the final bar.

Dynamics and phrasing: Apart from a few hairpins in ④ and ⑤, where fig-
ments of interest deserve encouragement, dynamics are closely related to
the original. It could be argued that the accompanying chords in bars 1-4
should be slurred across the bar line, but rhythmic precision may be improved with a soft-tongued attack on each chord. The long slurs in the cor
anglais and clarinet parts have been broken up into more manageable lengths.
In any case, what does Dvořák mean in bar 1, where the second and third
notes, being the same, cannot be slurred, and are certainly not to be tied?

Alternative instruments: With a group of this size, there are many possible
combinations.

a) ① and ② : trumpets

b) ③ : horn in F (transpose down a tone)

c) ④ and ⑤ : baritone and euphonium are interchangeable, and either
    part can be played by a trombone. The quaver arpeggio phrase in bar 9
    in ⑤ is based on one slide position and can be slurred, though care
    will be needed to avoid sounding the intervening C harmonic, lying be-
    tween G and E. For treble clef trombones, the parts can be played as
    they stand. For bass clef players the parts must be written down a
    major ninth at concert pitch.

d) ⑥ : in the absence of a E♭ bass, this part could be played by a eupho-
    nium. However, there would have to be some alterations to the given
    part, in order to stay within the instrument's range and to avoid cross-
    ing above ⑤. Study bars 3-8 in the following amended version, and
    compare it with the original E♭ bass part:

In a group of this size, there is no doubt that the euphonium would be
rather inadequate as the bottom instrument.

Score: This has been written out for brass band transposing instruments.
The use of alternative parts would involve transpositions as detailed
above.

Case Study 13: 'Folk Dance'

Very suitable for brass quartet, this little piece makes a good exercise in
staccato and sforzato attack in soft to loud playing.

Pitch: Concert pitch is down a tone from the original.

Range: All parts lie within the recommended range for trumpet and trombone.
In the last bar, to avoid playing very low in a forte passage, trumpet 2,
instead of taking the first trombone's notes as in bar 4, rises above the

final note of the first trumpet's melody. Some trombone slide positions
have been inserted to facilitate slurred intervals (see p 72).

Breathing: No melodic phrase is longer than four bars, and at the suggested speed it should be possible to play the piece as marked, with a breath
for the first trumpet at bar 8. On the ⌒ in the repeat at the end of
bar 10, trumpet 1 and trombone 2 should take the marked breath.

Alterations to the original: Three-note chords have been provided to
supply the rhythmic accompaniment, thus giving each player a part throughout the eleven-bar piece. Only at the beginning of the second half is the
trombone 2 melody doubled for three quavers by trombone 1.

Dynamics and phrasing: No significant dynamic alterations have been made,
apart from marking up the melody. Dynamics shown as mp/mf = 1st time/2nd
time.

Alternative instruments: a) ① and ② : cornets
                           b) ③ : tenor E♭ horn, baritone or euphonium
                           c) ④ : baritone or euphonium

Each pair of instruments could exchange parts at the repeats, making for
more interest for the performers.

SUMMARY

When arranging for brass, keep in mind the following points:

a) Suitability of music: for the beginner, the Renaissance and early
   Baroque repertoire of dances and chansons provides many suitable pieces —
   short, of limited compass and straightforward rhythm. Many of the collections made by Susato, Praetorius, and Attaingnant are readily available in modern editions, often arranged for recorders. For more advanced players, polyphonic music provides the added challenge of voice
   leading, independent movement, and more complex rhythmic figures.
   Classical and Romantic music, being largely string-based and less sec-
   tional, is not as suitable for brass, and piano music is generally not
   sympathetic and to be avoided. Imagine a Mozart Andante or a Chopin
   Nocturne played by a brass quartet, if you can! See pp 167-70 for
   suggested source material.

b) It is essential to appreciate the optimum ranges of all brass instruments. This is linked to the physical problems posed by playing high,
   loud, and long. Make sure that in an extended piece the performers get
   an occasional rest.

c) An appreciation of the potential of brass can be hastened by learning to
   play one of the easier instruments, such as the baritone or euphonium.
   One can only emphasize the value of practical experience.

Chapter V
Percussion: The instruments

While instruments of percussion are perhaps the oldest and most varied of all family groups, their place in composed music from about 1600 to the start of the present century has been neither very secure nor very important. Only the timpani have a continuous history, at first largely associated with trumpets. Oriental military instruments, such as the cymbal, bass drum, and triangle of the Turkish Janissary band, found their way into Western European music in the eighteenth century. However, in the last seventy-five years, the percussion section has grown and it now plays an important role in all types of music, while the influence of Carl Orff's educational methods have brought a new range of tuned and untuned percussion into the classroom.

There is now such a variety of instruments available that discussion will be reserved for only the most important and those whose notation and performing techniques are required knowledge.

CHARACTERISTICS

There are three basic groups of instruments:

a) Tunable - timpani, adjustable tambours, tambourines, and bongos.

b) Fixed pitch - chime bars, glockenspiels, metallophones, and xylophones.

c) Unpitched - cymbals, triangles, bells and jingles, maracas, castanets, side (or snare)-drums, and many more.

Tone and attack

One cannot generalize when there are so many different instruments. However, both tone and attack are largely dependent on the type of beater used and, in the case of many instruments, on the placing of the point of impact.

As an example, consider the large suspended cymbal. It can be struck at the edge, where the tone will be deep and largely focused on the lower partials. The sound will last a long time with a very gradual fade, unless the vibration is damped with the hand. On the bell (the dome which forms the centre of the cymbal) the tone is hard, emphasizing the upper partials. Here a note will quickly die. As might be expected, the sound elicited from a stroke at a point midway between the two extremes will contain a spread of harmonics, the sound fading fairly rapidly.

A large soft beater, such as an average timpani beater, will produce a sound very different from that made by a side-drum stick. A soft blow near the edge with a timpani beater gives a gong-like tone, while a hard blow results in a brilliant sound which encompasses not only low but many high harmonics. It is also possible to build up an effective crescendo with a

two-beater roll. The drier attack of a hard side-drum stick is useful for
emphasizing quiet rhythmic patterns. Again, tone varies with the strength
and position of the stroke, the bell producing a particularly hard metallic
sound.

Wire brushes elicit yet another type of sound, effective in quiet legato
music, while a triangle beater gives a hard ringing tone. One can stroke
the edge with a double bass bow or scrape the surface with a metal beater,
in each case producing a sound which can be heard only in thinly scored
music, or which may be used as a solo effect.

Composers and arrangers should be aware of these and other possibilities
and must write instructions into their scores relating to the type of
beater, the mode of attack, and whether the note should be stopped or
allowed to fade naturally — not forgetting the usual dynamic markings which,
in the case of percussion instruments, are particularly important. They
can be played quietly, and are often at their most effective when not used
in the context of a sfz situation. Beater in hand, the temptation to hit is
very strong. So, more often than not, is the resulting blow! Mark parts
clearly.

NOTATION

Staves: Tunable and fixed pitch instruments require a five-line stave with
bass and/or treble clefs, depending on the instrument. There is no firm
tradition for unpitched percussion. A single-line stave may be used, but
since scoring paper does not allow for this, it is customary, at least as
far as the score is concerned, to write one or more parts on a five-line
stave. How one disposes the parts can depend on a number of factors. Among
these are:

a) if a player is to perform on more than one instrument, both may be
   written on the same stave as, for example, side-drum and woodblock.
b) where high and low instruments can be accommodated, one at the top of the
   stave, the other at the bottom, tails must go in opposite directions —
   as for example, tenor and bass drum.
c) one five-line stave suffices for chime bar chords.

Clefs

a) Timpani are written in the bass clef.
b) Chime bars, glockenspiels, metallophones, and xylophones are written in
   the treble clef. The orchestral glockenspiel sounds two octaves above
   the written note, but the large number of similar school instruments may
   be treated rather differently, using a standard treble clef notation and

designating the type of instrument — soprano, alto/tenor, or bass — which
may involve concert pitch as written, or up or down an octave. In this
way children accustom themselves to one visual system.

Note-heads

Pitched instruments have normal note-heads. With unpitched percussion
there is no firm tradition, though normal note-heads are acceptable. In
order to differentiate between, for example, an edge stroke and a bell
stroke on the suspended cymbal, a normal note-head for the former and
for the latter can be used.

Ornamental strokes

The commonest are:

a) The roll: this may be measured or unmeasured.
   It is safest to write out a measured roll
   in full, or at least the first unit:

   For an unmeasured roll, two
   notations may be used:

Great care must be taken to notate accurately the end of any roll.

   If, in the example above, the last note is
   to be a separate single stroke, then write:

   If a fresh attack is to be made at
   the start of each bar, then write:

The same principles apply for other percussion instruments.

b) Side/snare-drum strokes

   flam : two stroke ruff/drag : three stroke ruff/drag

   The two stroke ruff may also be used by the timpani for single accented
   sf attacks.

Attack and duration

A strong attack is marked > or sfz.
A short dry note is marked , or if accented, .
It is important to remember that if a sustaining instrument is to play
short notes, these must be notated. For example, a triangle part might be
, whereas the non-sustaining xylophone could be written

 and the notes would last no longer than the hand-damped triangle in the first example (see p 95). The flam and ruff strokes (see p 84) are used for accented attacks on single notes or at the start of a roll.

Order of instruments in score

Apart from the timpani heading the orchestral percussion section, there is no established tradition.

THE INSTRUMENTS

Tunable

ORCHESTRAL TIMPANI: the standard pair give the following ranges:

The lowest and highest notes on each drum are the poorest in quality.

ORFF SCHOOL TIMPANI: in four sizes, covering a total range:

TUNABLE TAMBOURS and TAMBOURINES: in four sizes, each with a narrow range of about a minor third, within the bass stave.

Fixed pitch

CHIME BARS sound an octave higher than written pitch and a normal set gives a chromatic written range:

GLOCKENSPIELS, METALLOPHONES, and XYLOPHONES come in such a variety of size and range that only familiarity with what is available will ensure viable writing. Some are fully chromatic while others can be rigged to play in certain keys. On such an instrument the following passage is not possible:

A few technical points should be considered when writing for this group of instruments. Principally these involve the period of fade and the practical difficulties implied by a note pattern. Chime bars and the glockenspiel, if undamped, continue to ring and are therefore not suitable for rapid passage work. They should be used for held chords, and for supporting the harmony. The metallophone does not resonate to the same extent, while the xylophone is even drier and therefore more suited to any phrase where the underlying chordal structure is continually shifting.

With regard to note patterns, consider the alternation of left and right
hand beating. The following passages are easy:

Still representing a tonic-dominant progression, a re-ordering of the notes
presents real problems for the inexperienced player:

The problem of looking simultaneously at the music and the instrument is
a real one and there is no virtue in making difficult a passage which,
with a little thought, can be reduced to a left hand-right hand repeating
pattern. Equally, it seems to be easier to start a pattern with the left
rather than the right hand:

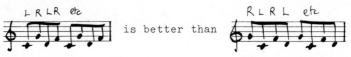

Ostinato patterns, either filling up the harmony or providing a bass line,
are the stock-in-trade of this group of instruments. The bass xylophone,
with its strong attack and well-defined tone, provides a good foundation
for junior ensemble work.

Unpitched

SIDE/SNARE-DRUMS come in different sizes and are played with the snares on
unless directed 'snares off'. Used mainly for pointing up the rhythm,
ostinati, and short crescendi, it is advisable to write plenty of notes,
as in Ravel's _Bolero_ ostinato:

The odd thwack is ineffective and better played on a larger drum, such as
the bass or tenor. Long practice is required to achieve a good roll, the
only means of sustaining a note. Know your player before you ask for the
impossible.

TAMBOURINE: Make sure that the method of playing is clearly marked. It
can be shaken, tapped with the fingers near the rim, or struck with the
flat of the hand at the centre. Shakes and rolls are shown in the normal
way:

   x=finger tap

CYMBALS are of many kinds and sizes. Possibilities with the suspended
cymbal have been discussed (see p 82). They may be clashed, and if the
resulting note is allowed to ring until it fades to nothing, this should
be indicated either verbally or by ♩ ⌣ . Otherwise a note should be
stopped according to its exact notated length.
Cymbals can make a lot of noise and the sound of continuous clashing soon
gets tiring. Other ways of using the instrument should be explored.

TRIANGLE: There are at least three different sizes. These should be specified, since general pitch is involved. The smallest triangle provides
little more than a tinkle while the largest, especially when trilled,
sounds not unlike a front door bell. Experiment with different beaters
and indicate your choice in the score. Don't over-use.

Other instruments, too many to list in full, provide sound effects —
sleigh bells and jingles, bird calls, rattles, and woodblocks for galloping
horses. Another group supply local colour - castanets, guiros, and tom-
toms.

EDUCATIONAL PERCUSSION
Beyond what has already been said and apart from the use of some of these
instruments in examples of junior ensemble music (see pp 93-102)
the specialized literature and repertoire for the full range of classroom
percussion is readily available elsewhere.

A final note
In the orchestra, band, or small ensemble, the musical effectiveness of
the percussion section is in inverse proportion to its use.

Chapter VI
Other instruments

This section lists those instruments not already mentioned which are likely
to be found in the school and youth club.

GUITAR (acoustic)

Apart from its use as a solo instrument or for accompanying singing, the
guitar can function as a bass or continuo 'filler' within the small
ensemble, most particularly with recorders and other soft-sounding instruments.

<u>Notation</u>

Standard notation is in the treble clef, the written notes sounding down
an octave. Various forms of tablature and chord symbols are also in current
use and often provide the most convenient way of indicating a 'filler' part,
the main role to which remarks will be directed.

The standard chord notation is:

   Major chords   - root position letter : C, G, E, etc

   Minor chords   - "   "   " + lower case 'm': Cm, Gm, Em, etc

   Dominant sevenths - "   "   " + 7: C7, G7, E7, etc

    In the case of a major seventh : Cma7, etc.

One of the advantages of this form of notation is that it avoids the need
to write the exact notes in any chord. Better players can manage fuller
chords, while the real beginner can concentrate on the single root note.

<u>Tuning</u>

written   sounding down an octave

<u>Suitable keys</u>

Because of the open string tuning, the major keys of A, D, G, and C and the
minor keys of D, E, and F♯ are easiest for basic chordal work — keys which
are equally suited to beginner violinists. Recorders like the keys of C,
G and F; the latter is not favoured by elementary guitarists. However, by
using a capo, effectively a movable transposing device, and by placing it
behind the first fret, F major can be fingered as E major. In this case,
notate as if for E major (nut position) and write in 'capo 1st fret'. The
capo allows a widening of the key range for the elementary guitarist in
the music-making of the classroom.

For examples see pp 90 and 93-5.

MELODICAS

Really a keyboard mouth organ, the melodica has found favour in educational
music for solo and group work.

Tone

The somewhat penetrating quality needs careful handling in combination with
recorder tone, but the larger melodicas can be successfully used as 'fill-
ers' with elementary violins.

Range

A number of models are available, the most commonly found having the following ranges. Notes in brackets are present only on more expensive models.

RECORDERS

Based on the Baroque pattern, today's mass-produced recorder is the most
widely used (and abused) junior school instrument. As easy to play badly
as it is difficult to play well, it can be musically effective in the
group situation, as indeed its Renaissance history as a consort instrument
proves. Recorders exist in a number of sizes, pitched a fifth and a fourth
apart. In the chart which follows, the lowest concert note and general
tonal characteristics are given for the five sizes of recorder which are
now easily available.

1) Sopranino (or octave): f" : very shrill

2) Descant (or soprano) : c" : bright

3) Treble (or alto)   : f' : the classical recorder of the 18th-century
                                 solo repertoire: good tone over the whole
                                 range.

4) Tenor   : c' : rather quieter than treble

5) Bass   : f : weak in tone, particularly the lowest notes:
                                 just sufficient to support the recorder
                                 consort.

Range

The bottom octave and a fifth provides the best playing compass; cross-
fingerings and intonation produce problems at the top end. The overall
range can be extended to just over two octaves by an accomplished player.

Notation

Unlike the cylindrical (closed pipe) Renaissance buzzers — crumhorn, kort-
holt, and rackett — the open-pipe recorder sounds an octave higher than the
equivalent reed instrument. Referring to the numbered recorders listed
above, the following notational conventions are widely established:

1) and 2) : written an octave below concert pitch

3)   : written at concert pitch

4) : written at concert pitch or an octave <u>above</u> concert pitch, using

either  or

5) : written in the bass clef, sounding <u>up</u> an octave.

Therefore the following chord  is notated

Suitable keys

The easiest keys are C, F, G and B♭. Keep this in mind when combining
recorders with other instruments. As an example, descant recorder and
guitar compromise best in G, D minor, and E minor.

This tune, equally possible on the treble recorder — in which case written
pitch sounds at concert pitch, not up an octave as with the descant
recorder — is also easy for the violin. The guitar's simple chordal
accompaniment will give adequate support to any or all of the suggested
instruments.

Recorder repertoire is extensive and easily available.

PIANO

Useful as it is to give moral support and to accompany singing and instrumental solos, the piano does not blend well and it should be looked upon
as a means to an end and not as a refuge for the unconfident teacher to
hide behind. It stands not only as a visual barrier but as a tonal
barrier between the player and everyone else. Furthermore, once children
have come to rely on it, they tend not to fend for themselves. Therefore,
use with discretion.

Part 2
Arranging for groups: Introduction

One case study in each chapter will concern the same source material, the carol 'We've been awhile a-wandering', (<u>Carols for Choirs I</u>, London, 1961, p 158). This will make it possible to compare characteristic arrangements for each type of instrumental group. The tune, as barred by its collector, Ralph Vaughan Williams, is given here:

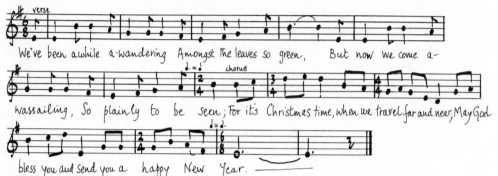

The numerous changes in time signature and the equating of $\downarrow$. with $\downarrow$ as the value of the beat have been variously altered in the arrangements which follow, in an attempt to simplify the metrical problems inherent in the melody. It has also been transposed down a tone into D minor, a key more suited to the majority of instruments.

By using the arrangements 'end-on', it would be possible to employ four different instrumental groups for any of the six verses, thus providing the junior ensemble, the concert wind band, the brass band, and the orchestra of a large school the opportunity to participate in a single carol at the Christmas concert. As the harmonies are different in each arrangement, it is not musically possible to superimpose one version on top of another.

The short <u>Song</u> by Gibbons (see pp 2 and 52-4) will be used again to illustrate technical problems of chord spacing and balance. The remaining case studies are of various types and styles. They include examples of reduction, expansion, and translation, and each will be analysed in terms of instrumentation, texture, bowing and so on.

At this point, a re-reading of Chapter I (pp 1-9) is advised, since it has particular significance for what is to follow.

Chapter VII
Arranging for junior ensemble

GENERAL PRINCIPLES

A junior music group generally includes melody instruments, tuned percussion, and guitars to fill in the harmony and, with luck, a bass instrument.
Extra percussion can be added as available.

The instrumentation in the case studies which follow is based on such a
group. Not all the instruments are essential to a performance, a point
which should be considered, since junior groups have a tendency to expand
or contract, depending on the weather and the health of the participants.
In the same way, scoring should be designed to work as well with the few
as with the many. All children should be encouraged to perform, and very
simple parts for the not so musically gifted should be included, whether
for open strings or for some innocuous percussion instruments. Participa-
tion is much more important than subtle attempts at balancing the constituent elements of the score in matters of dynamics, voice leading, and
general musical finesse.

CASE STUDIES

Case Study 14: Carol 'We've been awhile a-wandering'

The first arrangement of this carol is designed for classroom use. Some
parts are optional, others, particularly untuned percussion, could be
added to the chorus, copying the rhythm of the guitar part. The verse is
based on a two-bar ostinato which breaks down in the chorus, due to the
rhythmic structure of the melody. The whole piece has been set out in
common time. Once the idea of triplets is understood, there should be
no problem in performance.

No dynamics have been inserted. The unknown strength and balance of
players and instruments in a class, not to mention the possible addition
of singers, leaves the problem to be solved in each rehearsal and performance.

The score follows a generally accepted pattern, with melody instruments at
the top and chord instructions at the bottom, making it possible to provide
an ad lib piano accompaniment should circumstances require.

We've been awhile a-wandering

trad. Yorkshire carol

Note the following points:

INSTRUMENTATION

All melody instruments double the tune — melodicas, descant recorders, and
violins; there is safety in numbers! Additional treble recorder parts
would have to be written up an octave.

Strings are in first position throughout. The violin bowing suggested is
preferred, but very elementary players might have to use alternate bows in
the verse.

Chime bars: a one-octave set (written c' - c'') will suffice; B♮ is used
throughout. A glockenspiel is an obvious alternative. Four chords are

used, and E, F, G, and A are common to
two chords. This being the case,
separate parts can be written for
four pairs of hands. Opposite is
the two-bar ostinato scored for
four players:

If sufficient chime bars are available, three players could be assigned
to each of the four chords, thus allowing for twelve players in all.

Guitar: the part is designed for the chordal type of player, whose competence will determine the specific notes in each chord. Rapid changes, as
in bar 8, can be simplified by the omission of one chord.

Minimum forces required: recorder or violin or melodica — and bass xylophone or cello or guitar — and chime bars (glockenspiel) or guitar.

Parts for any number of other instruments could be added. For example, a
small xylophone might double the tune. Its drier sound is most suited to
the fast stepping melody, the clarity of which would be blurred if played
on any form of chime.

Supposing clarinets were available, what sort of part might they be given?
Take the tune first. Does it lie within one register or across the 'break'?
The answer is that at transposed written pitch it moves from a' to b' in
almost every bar, a most awkward progression. Obviously a filler part,
perhaps following the lowest chime bar line, would be more suitable for
the elementary player.

NOTATION

Compare the cello's 𝅗𝅥 𝄾𝅘𝅥 with the bass xylophone's 𝅘𝅥𝄾𝄾𝅘𝅥 , an instance
where it is pointless to write a minim when the tone fades quickly. If
more sound is required of the bass xylophone, then write 𝅘𝅥𝅘𝅥𝄾𝅘𝅥 .

Case Study 15: Microdanse - Hommage à B.B., for two pianos

Children's piano music based on ostinato figures often provides a suitable
starting point for a short piece for junior ensemble. In its original form,
this dance can be performed either as a duet for two pianos or as two separate solos, using either piano I or piano II. In the arrangement, essential melodic lines are marked I and II, corresponding to the original piano
parts.

GENERAL PRINCIPLES

The arrangement, like the original, is intended to be flexible. Many parts
are optional and, where necessary, the music has been altered in detail to
suit the technique of elementary performers.

The main elements of this piece are:

    bars 1-16: ostinato bass (II LH) and quaver movement (mainly I LH)

    bars 1-8 : canonic melody (I and II RH)

    bars 9-12: melody in tenor (I LH) with accompanying dialogue (I and II
            RH)

    bars 13-16: coda with thickened texture

In any arrangement, particular attention must be given to these essential
musical components. Look for them in the following version:

MICRODANSE : Hommage à B.B.

INSTRUMENTATION

The original two-piano score (I and II) has been translated so that it can
be played in a number of different ways. A general point should first be
made about the cello 1 and double bass parts. The latter, a very simple
open-string part, may be taken by a cello if no bass is available. The
tenor melody in bars 9-12 (piano I LH), which follows the ostinato in outline, is doubled in cello 1 and violin 3 (or viola). Therefore if there is
only one cellist, he is advised to play the double bass part when violin 3
or viola are available. If there are only two violins and one cellist, the
latter should play the cello 1 part. A second cello could then play the
double bass part.

For piano I, the minimum forces are:

  Strings only: violins 1 and 3 (or viola) and a cello on the double bass
  part.

  Wind and percussion only: descant recorder 1, clarinet, and xylophone 1 —
  preferably a small instrument to match the 4ft tone of the recorder, which
  sounds an octave higher than written. The clarinet is the only wind instrument given the tenor melody in bars 9-12. A three-note ostinato, re-
  written in the treble clef from the double bass part, would sound well on
  a bass xylophone.

Obviously a mixture of strings, wind, and percussion is also possible: descant recorder 1, clarinet, a xylophone to maintain the quaver movement, and
a cello on the double bass part.

For pianos I and II, the minimum forces are:

  Strings only: violins 1 and 2, violin 3 (or viola) and double bass (or
  cello). If there is no violin 3 or viola to play the melody in bars 9-12,
  then two cellos (or one cello and double bass) could cover the essential
  material (cello I and double bass parts).

  Wind and percussion only: as before, with the addition of descant recorder 2.

Optional instruments: flute, trumpet, xylophone 2, and cello 2.

Any mixed combination of I and II will serve as, for example, violins 1 and
2 to I, all recorders to II. This order is suggested, since it allows the
recorders the second entry of the canon at the higher octave, thus providing an echo effect. It also places the two interlocking parts in bars 9-12
nearer to one another in pitch.

Extra percussion can be added as desired. Two tambours or chime bars tuned
to D and A could play a simplified ostinato. Simarly, a guitar might fill
this role, playing chords until bar 11. In bar 12 a chord of A major
would sound C# against C♮. To avoid this, a pedal D should be played through

the last five bars.

Taking the rhythmic figures ♩♩𝅗𝅥 and 𝄾♩𝅗𝅥 from the flute and trumpet parts, untuned percussion could also be added to the score in bars 1-8, and again in bars 13-16, where repeated minims would be more appropriate.

TECHNIQUE AND STYLE

Strings

Violins and violas: all parts are in first position throughout. The upper two parts are largely scalic. While the use of the fourth finger is not strictly necessary, it has been suggested in a few instances.

Cellos and double bass: all parts are very simple. The only problem is in cello I in bar 10, where a shift is necessary to take the high E. To keep the part in first position, an alternative lower E is given. The leaping pizzicato provides a contrast to the stepping upper melodic lines and helps to lighten the texture.

Bowing: the easiest bowing has been given. Players able to use the fourth finger with confidence could take four quavers in one bow. The middle parts have been bowed in paired crotchets to emphasize the main beats, but notice the greater activity in the last four bars, where alternate bows help to achieve the crescendo. In bars 10 and 11 the viola's quavers are not slurred, so avoiding awkward string crossing at speed. This problem does not arise in the doubled part on violin 3 and cello 1. In the last bar, lifting the bow off the first beat for a down-bow on the final note will add the required emphasis implied in the original piano II part.

Wind

Recorders: the parts lie well within the range of young players. They are not suited to the treble recorder; written up an octave, they would be too high. Very elementary descant players could manage the flute part, written down an octave.

Flute: though it lies wholly within the second register, this is an easy part.

Clarinet: the key signature is rather forbidding, but the part is all below the 'break'. When there is a full string section, the part is optional.

Trumpet: sharps have been added into the part to help the beginner. A second clarinet could play this line, which would need some rewriting if it is to avoid crossing the 'break' in the last five bars.

Percussion: the size of xylophones has not been stipulated. If all strings are playing, then alto/tenors would serve well: if only recorders, sopranos would be preferable. The first part is the easier, since the left hand plays on the beat and has the moving part (see p 85). Notice the key sig-

nature, which applies strictly to the notes played. Glockenspiels would be
too resonant for this fast moving part.

SUMMARY

This dance is a good example of a piece which can be made to work well with
elementary players. Why? It has an ostinato bass throughout, allowing
repetitive note patterns for the beginner. The melodic material, half of
which is optional and can be dispensed with if good players are short, is
based largely on scales and, in the original key, lies very well for
strings.

The range is also good for descant recorders, and the repetitive ♪♪♩ and
𝄾 ♩. ♩ figures lend themselves to the wind player who has been learning for
a bare fortnight.

Above all, it is lively and short.

Chapter VIII
Arranging for small mixed ensemble

GENERAL PRINCIPLES

In some ways, this is the most difficult assignment, where balance, texture,
and tone-colour have to be carefully weighed up. Other important points
an arranger must consider are:

a) Key: this depends largely on the constitution of the group. The final
   choice is generally a compromise.

b) Range: for good effect, write in the best range of each instrument.

c) Character and style must, as far as possible, be suited to the instruments available.

d) The score is easiest to read if the formal pitch order is maintained -
   soprano instruments at the top and bass instruments at the bottom of
   the system.

The Song by Gibbons again provides us with a short piece which will enable
analysis of some of these points, as well as the problem of chord spacing.

CASE STUDIES
Case Study 16: Song no 46 by Orlando Gibbons

Let us suppose that we have the following group: two clarinets, viola,
E♭ tenor horn, and trombone. Though the clarinet can be considered as a
soprano instrument, the general range of the given group is middle to low.
What about the key? Unlike the violin, the viola is happy playing in up
to two flats, and the other instruments definitely favour the keys of B♭
and E♭ . Looking first at the piece in its original key of F, it is
obvious that the clarinet - or two clarinets doubling at the unison — will
find the melody lying awkwardly across the weakest part of its range:

The viola, the only other instrument capable of playing the tune at its
original pitch, would never balance the remaining four instruments. However one arranges the parts underneath, the result is likely to be unsatisfactory. Supposing we now transpose the piece down a fifth into B♭, this
would allow the clarinets to play either above or below the 'break', with

the exception of bar 5, where the upper part is:
However, the second clarinet doubling an octave
below will strengthen the tune at this point.

Assume, therefore, that we try the piece in B♭, with the melody doubled at
the octave. How would the other instruments manage, and how would the alto
and tenor parts be distributed, assuming that the trombone is bound to play
the bass line?

The viola would have to take the alto part, since the tenor goes below its
range unless alterations are made to the inner part-writing. Even so, the
viola uses only the bottom two strings. The tenor part also lies low for
the horn. The lowest notes of the trombone are rather weak and indistinct
and if these are to be avoided, some will have to be transposed up an
octave.

In the various arrangements which follow, repeated notes in the accompanying harmony have been tied to allow the melody to stand clear and, in the
case of the brass, for the added reason that it is not easy to articulate
cleanly at the bottom of the range. In bar 2, notice the trombone slur.
This only involves a shift from 1st to 2nd position, and it comes on a
suspension. The slur is both technically feasible and musically desirable.
The same might be said of the viola part in bar 6.

What is wrong with the above arrangement? The main trouble is that in
bars 5 and 6 those notes in the trombone part marked **x** lie above the tenor
line. This upsets the harmony, creating three 'awkward' second inver-
sions. While the positions of upper and middle parts may be reversed,
this is not permissible with a bass part.

The melody should stand clear, being doubled by clarinet 1 playing up the
octave, but with most instruments playing at the bottom of their range,

the over-all sound will be rather dull. How can we get round these problems?

If the piece is to remain in B♭, we can try moving the tenor part up an
octave, giving it to the viola, while the horn takes the alto line at its
present pitch. This would leave the clarinets and trombone as before:

We have now solved the problem of the bass crossing above the tenor line.
Both tenor horn and viola now play within a more convenient range, and it
would be possible to interchange clarinet 2 and viola parts. Whichever
instruments play the melody, the overall sound should be an improvement on
the previous arrangement, and the fact that a middle part lies above the
lower octave melody is of little significance.

However, as with the previous arrangement, objection on harmonic grounds
can be made to the progression from bar 5 to bar 6, where all parts leap up.
If the trombone moved down to low G in bar 6, then the same offence would
be committed between that chord and the next one, and the trombone cannot
go down again to low D, which is beyond its range.
The solution is to move the trombone up to high
B♭ in bar 5, and to alter the tenor horn part so
that it still lies above the new bass-line:

Another possibility would be to transfer the tune into the tenor range,
making a 'faux-bourdon' type of arrangement. To project the melody, the
tenor horn would have to be the principal, partnered by a clarinet playing
in unison. The original alto part is now taken up an octave on the viola,
while the tenor goes to the top where it lies very comfortably for the first
clarinet. The problem alluded to above concerning chord progressions in
bars 5 and 6 now involves a new top part with the trombone, and the solution

will therefore be different. Here is
the given tenor line, now acting as a
descant, with the bass:

The suggested amendment is given in the full arrangement below. It could
be argued that the resulting chord, with only one B$^\flat$, is unbalanced, but
this is preferable to the awkward harmonic progression shown above. Here,
then, is the 'faux-bourdon' version of the piece:

Nothing has been said about dynamics. The piece is probably best played
rather quietly, especially if associated with the poem by Phineas Fletcher:
'Drop, drop, slow tears', as in The English Hymnal (no 98). In each
arrangement a general marking, say mp, should ensure a reasonably balanced
sound, the melody predominating a little because of the extra instrument
on this line. Much will depend on the skills of individual players. A
reticent viola may need encouraging with an mf, an exuberant horn player
might equally require gentle restraint with a p.
With regard to phrasing, an attempt to allow the melody to stand out
naturally has been made by not slurring this part. With the exception
already noted, the trombone cannot achieve a true slur at the technical
level at which this piece is aimed. Inner parts have been bowed or
slurred as is compatible with a legato chordal accompaniment. A general
instruction 'slow and smoothly' might well be added to score and parts.

It is hoped that the process of 'thinking through' a simple arrangement
like this tune will have helped to highlight some of the problems involved.

Case Study 17: Interlude based on the carol 'We've been awhile a-wandering'

The musical material on which this miniature is based derives from the
arrangements of the carol: see case studies on pp 93, 113, 128, and 136.
In comparison with Case Study 16, basically an accompanied tune, here frag-
ments of melody and rhythmic figures are tossed about the group, first one
instrument, then another taking the lead. The texture is therefore quite
different, and more attention has been paid to each instrument's character
and tonal individuality. Detailed points will be discussed in the analysis
following the piece:

Key: D minor, common to subsequent arrangements, has been retained here,
suiting all wind and providing few problems (F and B♭) for the violin and
none for the cello. The piece is within the range of technically limited
performers, though there is ample opportunity for subtle phrasing.

Characteristic writing: Flute, clarinet, and violin are treated equally as
regards pitch, each in turn emerging to take the highest part. The horn
calls in bars 3 and 10 suggest the historical open note fourth and fifth
intervals associated with the instrument in its pre-valve days. Its low
notes provide the bass-line below the cello in bars 6-7. Elsewhere the
horn is used to complete the harmony, a function which suits it better
than playing the little rhythmic figure given to the top three instruments.
Open string pizzicato notes on the cello help to lighten the texture, and
the bowing in bar 4 has been so arranged to make possible a rapid change
to pizzicato in bar 5.

As far as possible, each instrument has been given an interesting part,
the cello alone having no clear melodic statement.

Blend and contrast: At the start the clarinet, then the flute and the
horn should be clearly heard. With the violin, each in turn have entries
of either melodic or rhythmic significance. In the fully scored sections,
the horn has been kept low so as not to protrude where blend is more important than the tonal contrast so essential at the beginning of the piece.

Dynamics: In this generally quiet piece, there is little need to differentiate dynamic markings between loud and soft sounding instruments,
though an attempt has been made to grade dynamics according to the importance of a particular phrase.

Score: The placing of the horn immediately above the cello makes it easier
to read the score, which would be confusing if the traditional orchestral
order had been followed.

Band parts should be adequately cued, as follows:

Supposing this piece were to be re-scored for wind quintet — flute, oboe,
clarinet, horn, and bassoon — what changes would have to be made to the
score? Oboe to violin part; slurs to remain: bassoon to cello part;
remove pizz/arco marks, adding dim ($\Longrightarrow$) to all former pizz notes; slur
second and third notes in bar 4: score layout to standard wind quintet
form — invert present clarinet and violin parts. Musically the result
would be possible; the original conception of the cello writing would
suffer most, in the transfer to a bassoon.

Case Study 18: Helston Furry Dance

The opportunity to meet the challenge offered by the words of the chorus of
'The Furry Dance' is too great to pass up. Here we have 'fiddle, cello,
big bass drum; bassoon, flute, and euphonium' in an arrangement of the
piece. Technically it is not difficult, since the fast passages are based
on straightforward scales.

Key: This is suited to all save the euphonium, whose part is purposely less
busy.

Range: All important material is within the best range of each instrument.
Follow the melody line: bars 1-4 bassoon and cello: bars 5-8 flute: bars
9-12 euphonium: bars 13-16 flute and violin. Apart from the drummer, each
player has a share in the tune.

Characteristic writing: The treatment of the melodic line has already
been mentioned. The violin's pizzicato chords in bars 1-4 on the off-beat
are easy, with an open string A common to all. The drum both 'ooms' and
'pahs', adding extra force at the end with ♪♪♩ strokes.

Blend and contrast: With a group of such diverse tonal character, no
attempt has been made to achieve blend. Apart from the last four bars,
the main impression is one of contrast in pitch and timbre: bars 1-4 low
pitch, heavy weight, the euphonium providing the bass line: bars 5-8
high pitch, light weight, only two parts: bars 9-12 flute adds a touch of
brightness to the heavy euphonium tune: bars 13-16 everybody plays. The
over-all impression is one of contrast.

Texture: Harmonically very simple, the texture of the arrangement also
supports the idea of contrast - four parts in bars 1-4 and only two in
bars 5-8. In the second half, the reverse applies: in bars 9-12 the
tenor melody is supported by bassoon and drum, with the flute, violin,
and cello filling in the harmony with rhythmic points. In the last four
bars the crescendo is supported by a general increase in activity.
Notice, for example, the bassoon part, both more agile than the cello
and, where possible, extending an octave below it. Here for the only
time the tune is doubled at the upper octave by the flute, which greatly
strengthens the line.

Character and style: As befits the continuing use of this tune for the
Cornish 'Furry Dance', the arrangement is somewhat rustic and rumbustious
and attempts an imitation of the improvised village band.

Dynamics: The foregoing remarks cover general dynamic levels. Within
each section, some attempt has been made to produce the desired effect.
For example, the bass drum is marked down throughout, and in bars 9-12
the elementary bass line given to the bassoon is marked up to balance the
euphonium.

SUMMARY

The three case studies in this section were designed to illustrate problems general to arranging all music for small ensemble — key, range, and
so on. Stylistically they are very varied. Gibbons's Song is a straight
harmonization of a melody for elementary players. The Interlude is composed for specific players and is therefore tailor-made and instrumentally
conceived from the first. Lastly, the 'Furry Dance' makes the best of an
odd lot in an attempt to re-create the village band. Many lessons can be
learned from a study of the musical material and the accompanying
analyses. What are the most important points?

More often than not in the school or youth group situation one is con-
fronted by a collection of players of varied performing standards on a
mixture of instruments. Faced with the problem of providing suitable
material for a group, the first thing an arranger must do is to assess
the various capabilities of its members. Having chosen an appropriate
piece, he must then go through the process outlined in the discussion on
the Song, considering the best key, optimum ranges and, so far as is
possible, instrumental colour, contrasts of texture, rhythmic accompanying
figures, and other musical points.

Always try to see a piece from the point of view of the individual player.
Note-spinning is tedious, so try to give everyone an interesting part
with some element of challenge — a small solo or an important rhythmic
figure. The success of an arrangement can only be gauged by performance,
and there is no substitute for practical experience gained by trial and
error. Write, play, listen, revise.

Chapter IX
Arranging for orchestra

GENERAL PRINCIPLES

Orchestras vary in size, in skill, and in the balance of strength between
family groups. Nowhere is this more evident than in school, college, and
youth orchestras, where factors far removed from musical considerations
may affect the constitution of what, for want of a better description, is
called 'the orchestra'.

For practical reasons, however, limits must be set. These will be taken
as those governing the standard 'small orchestra' — one or two flutes,
oboe, two clarinets, bassoon, two trumpets, horn, trombone, strings, and
percussion.

To allow for the inevitable hazards already mentioned, adequate cueing of
the less common instruments is essential, and there is much to be said
for designing an arrangement so that it can be performed by either strings
or woodwind alone or by a mixture of the two, while the brass are scored
as an optional extra. This imposes a strict discipline on the arranger,
but utility scoring of this type, aimed at the performing ability with
which we are concerned, is not only desirable but often essential. The
case studies will show how it can be done.

One other general point: the three-year wind player will be more advanced
technically than his string-playing contemporary, so it is important to
score accordingly. Forget the eighteenth-century type of score in which
strings carry the brunt of the argument, with occasional asides and glosses
from the wind.

CASE STUDIES

Case Study 19: Carol 'We've been awhile a-wandering'

GENERAL PRINCIPLES

The melody of this carol, quoted on p 92, has been transposed down a tone
into D minor/F major, a key more suited to the various arrangements (see
pp 93, 128, and 136). Since all instruments here play in compound time
in the verse section — compare with version on p 94 — $\frac{12}{8}$ is considered the
most suitable time-signature.

As already mentioned, the arrangement may be played by strings or woodwind
alone. If it were to be used with voices, then the first and last verses
might be tutti, the intervening four verses alternating strings and wind.
All could join together for the chorus. This would allow the wind an
occasional breather, as they would find six repeats very exhausting.
Detailed discussion of cueing is held over until the analysis.

Carol: 'We've been awhile a-wandering'

INSTRUMENTATION AND CUED PARTS: The following instructions clarify the
use of cued parts:

Performing group	Essential cues (marked in parts — vn/tpt 1 etc.)
woodwind only	all
woodwind and brass	string
strings	flute

If no viola, either transfer part to violin 3 (not included in score),
transposing bars 3-6 up an octave, or use cue for divisi cello. The bass
doubles the cello and could be omitted, with the loss of 16ft tone, sounding down an octave.

To cover the possible absence of any one instrument, every essential
melodic and harmonic line is doubled. For example the bassoon, not the
most readily available instrument, is covered variously by cello, clarinet
2, and viola. As far as is possible, each instrument has been given an
interesting part, the thematic material being well shared. Follow through
each part in the arrangement and see if its omission would seriously compromise the overall effect. This does not mean to say that a full complement will not prove more satisfactory nor, in the case of a 'flu epidemic,
that one can survive musically with one violin and a trombone. But one
can take precautions.

STYLE AND TEXTURE: These are largely conditioned by what has already been
said about the nature of the arrangement. Everything depends on how it is
used, but assuming a full orchestra, contrast is the obvious characteristic,
alternating strings, woodwind — with or without brass — and tutti in the
various verse and chorus sections.

The verse is harmonized in four parts. In the chorus, the strings are in
three essential parts, but woodwind and brass add extra lines. In a tutti
version of the chorus, therefore, the melody is heard over three octaves —
flute and violin 1 above high voices; clarinet 1, trumpet 1, and violin 2
with high voices; horn with low voices, except for the last few notes
which lie too low. Bassoon, cello, and double bass support the various
inner parts — oboe, clarinet 2, trumpet 2, trombone, and viola. The
doubling of top and bottom parts is essential in a full orchestra score
of this type, particularly the upper octave version of the melody, which
might otherwise be submerged by the loud middle-range brass.

Dynamics have been added on the assumption that the arrangement will be
used in conjunction with voices, the verses sung by a choir of high or low
voices, with everyone joining in the chorus. Inner harmony parts have been
marked down in the introduction and verse.

TECHNICAL POINTS

Strings: except for violin 1, parts are in first position.

a) Fingering: violins in bars 1 and 2: A fingered 4 to avoid string
   crossing under slur. Shifts of position in violin 1 in chorus section
   are fingered.

b) Bowing: the $\frac{12}{8}$ melody ideally requires the given slurred group
   staccato ♩♪♩♪.   Alternate bowing, easier for beginners, brings
   with it the problem of running out of bow or, alternatively, 'bumping'
   every quaver in a scramble to get back to the heel (see pp 18-19).
   Which type of bowing is used will often depend not so much on musical
   considerations as on the technical competence of the performers.
   In the louder chorus section, alternate bowing is specified - more
   movement means more sound.
   The pizzicato double bass part in bars 1 and 2 adds rhythmic point
   without weight. The bowed chorus section provides sufficient foundation tone to support the full orchestra.

Woodwind: Technically there are few problems. The chorus melody lies
awkwardly for clarinet 1, but it has been transposed up at the climax:
'a happy New Year'. If the clarinet was the only instrument on the tune
this would be serious, but it is adequately reinforced, particularly by
trumpet 1.

Brass: Compare the phrasing of the horn and trombone in bars 3 and 4.
Whereas true slurring is possible on the former, the trombone has been
marked legato to encourage soft tonguing. Notice trumpet 1's short
counter-melody in bars 5-6, and the horn part in bar 9 where, to avoid
the awkward downward leap of a seventh, the melody steps up a tone, the
leap being taken on the easier c''-c' open note octave. The trombone is
treated throughout as a tenor voice.

Percussion: Abandoning its traditional tonic-dominant function in the
modulating chorus section, the timpani's D and A have to serve as best
they can in a passage which passes through A minor, D minor, F major, and
back to D minor. Study the drum part in bars 9 and 10.

Case Study 20:   Sarabande from Suite no 6 — (Consorts for four viols) —
                                                    by Matthew Locke

GENERAL PRINCIPLES

Two versions are given of the opening section of Locke's piece. The first
is another utility arrangement, with the built-in safeguards found in the
previous case study. This type of scoring can be seen as superimposed
arrangements for family groups, producing terraced tone colour if strings
and woodwind are used alternately in repeated material. The second version
is an example of mixed scoring, more related to the small ensemble genre.
Here one may find shifting tone colour, with instruments overlapping in
their entries to produce a subtler and ever changing sound pattern.

Case Study 20a

In this first version, the piece may be performed by strings alone; Locke's
original viol parts are retained for violins 1 and 2, viola and cello. If
the cues to the brass are used (bars 17-19), then the woodwind cover between them all the composer's material. Assuming a full complement is
available, the best way to treat an arrangement of this type is to alter
the orchestration either at repeats or by smaller sections, particularly
suitable in this Sarabande. In this way tonal variety is achieved and the
wind get a rest. Two schemes for performance are proposed:

a) Treating the piece

by section (repeats)	1st time	2nd time
bars 1-12	tutti	strings
13-24	woodwind and brass	strings
2nd time bar 29	tutti	

b) Treating the piece

by phrase		
bars 1-4	tutti	woodwind
5-8	woodwind	strings
9-12	strings and brass	tutti
13-16	woodwind	strings
17-20	brass	brass
middle of 20-24	tutti	strings and brass
2nd time bar 29	tutti	

MUSICAL STYLE: Certain aspects of seventeenth-century style and performing
traditions have to be considered in making an arrangement of this piece.
This is not the place to enter into a detailed discussion of the influence

on English music of the French practice of playing paired quavers unequally, but it probably applies to this Sarabande. Ornamentation is also a problem; the shake ($\mathcal{W}$) is found in the original, while editorial additions such as the obvious trill in bar 11 have been added in square brackets.[1] Of more immediate importance is the rhythmic accentuation across the bar-line — hemiola. This is a common feature of Baroque music, which affects bowing and phrasing in general.

a) <u>Hemiola</u> is the telescoping of two bars of $\frac{3}{4}$ into one bar of $\frac{3}{2}$, so that accents occur in different parts of the $\frac{3}{4}$ bars concerned:

Hemiola usually happens at the lead into a cadential point, as in bars 2-3, 10-11, 14-15, 18-19, and 22-23. It might be advisable to bracket

in the band parts in order to clarify the accentuation.

b) <u>Texture</u>: there is much musical argument in this piece. Sometimes it is concealed within the inner parts. Take, for example, the motif in violin 2 at bar 5. Beginning on the third beat, the cello imitates it in each of bars 5-7 and 9. The viola has it in bars 8 and 9, starting on the third beat. This rising third permeates the whole texture, and an attempt has been made in the woodwind writing to illuminate this detail.

c) <u>Dynamics</u>: all markings are editorial. A blanket system has been used, <u>f</u> or <u>mp</u> in all parts, which is the most suitable approach for the piece in an arrangement of this nature.

TECHNICAL POINTS

<u>Strings</u>

<u>Bowing</u>: Apart from the particular example of hemiola, many of the bowing problems associated with triple time occur in this piece. Where there are three crotchets in a bar, either the first or the last two must be slurred or taken in one bow if the next bar is to start with a down-bow. Assuming an accent on the first beat of the bar and therefore a long stroke, it is best to take the last pair of notes on an up-bow. On the other hand where, in bars 5-9, one finds , it is preferable to lift off the first note with an up-bow, placing the down-bow on the accented minim.

___

[1]Further information can be found in the modern critical edition: Matthew Locke, <u>Chamber Music II</u>, Musica Britannica vol XXXII (London, 1972)

Case Study 20a: Sarabande (Suite no 6 - consorts for 4 viols) by

Matthew Locke

* slurred ⌢ only
for first time bar

Throughout, musical considerations have conditioned the bowing, and in this respect the piece repays careful study. Notice, for example, how the first quaver in bars 2 and 3 in violin 1 has to be played on the same bow, yet separated from the preceding long note:

The need for the down-bow indicated in bar 13 arises from the repeat at bar 24, where the final note is also taken with a down-bow. A small problem exists in the bowing at the first time bar, where one must slur across the bar-line. However, if going straight on to the second time bar, this is not the case, and the altered phrasing must be indicated in all parts concerned.

For the last section, where the music is spacious and loud, alternate long bows should be used.

Woodwind

Here we have five instruments to share four parts. This allows both for rests and for the opportunity to add to Locke's original where appropriate, particularly from bar 21 to the end. For instance, in imitation of the quaver thirds in bar 20 (flute and clarinet 1), clarinet 2 has been given a matching entry in bar 21.

In this closing section, violin 1 has a telescoped entry of the main theme in bar 24, the first note of the second entry being omitted. This has been restored in clarinet 1. In the same way, the off-beat entry first clearly heard in violin 1 and which is disguised in the viola part in bar 27, has been identified in the oboe entry, reinforced by the trombone, and finally repeated by the horn in bar 28.

The legitimacy of tinkering with Locke's original four-part score can be challenged. However, this is an arrangement, not a transcription.

Brass

References to the treatment of the music in the closing bars has already been made. Elsewhere, the three instruments are used to strengthen the two main cadences (bars 10-12 have additional parts) and only in bars 17-20, in the low pitched trio, do they predominate. Indeed, they might be allowed to play this phrase on their own. Notice that the shakes (⌇) have been omitted, being inappropriate to the instruments in question.

Shakes: Most shakes are playable. The most difficult is in bar 19 ── violin 2, involving the fourth finger or a shift of position.

Case Study 20b

The second version of bars 1-12 of Locke's Sarabande sets out to show how
this four-part piece can be orchestrated in such a way that instrumental
colour is used to point melodic and rhythmic motifs. Only woodwind and
strings are used in this short section. Particular attention has been
drawn to the ♩ 𝅝 phrase, entries on the beat being doubled at the octave —
clarinet 2 with violins and flute with oboe. The bass entries are shared
between cello and bassoon, joining together with the double bass only for
the last entry in bar 9. Wherever possible, the phrase drops a fourth to
overlap the next entry, so preventing a chopped-up effect. After the first
four-bar phrase, which is self-contained, the music should run through to
the climax at the cadence in bar 12. The overlapping assists this sense
of continuity.

MUSICAL STYLE
The main features have already been discussed.

a) Texture: in bars 1-4 the scoring is light; pairs of woodwind and
   strings, while the plucked double bass emphasizes the cadence. The
   interesting bars are 5-9, where the texture provides touches of sound
   from all the instruments in turn. Only in the last three bars do all
   the instruments play.

b) Dynamics are editorial. Note the phrasing off of the last note in the
   ♩ 𝅝 │𝅝 ♪│ motif, so as not to obscure the next entry. Important lines
   have been marked up, as the viola in bars 5-8 and the imitative clarinet
   1 in bars 7-9.

TECHNICAL POINTS
There is little to add to comments already made. Notice the flute in bars
10-11. To avoid clumsy cross-fingerings and awkward ornamentation, the
part has been simplified compared with the original version an octave below
in violin 1.

Sarabande (Suite no 6 - Consorts for 4 viols) by Matthew Locke

SUMMARY

The arrangements in this section have attempted to show how to tackle
three different problems. The carol is a free arrangement of a given
melody, while the first version of the Sarabande is the expansion of a
four-part piece for orchestra, with minimal additional harmony notes,
mainly confined to the brass. It is also a translation from strings to
wind. Both arrangements incorporate cross-cueing and other safety features,
often so essential in the school or youth club situation.

On the other hand, Case Study 20b demonstrates a more sophisticated
approach, demanding the presence and self-reliance of each instrumentalist,
particularly among the woodwind.

Finally, much of what was said on p 112 applies equally here.

Chapter X
Arranging for brass band

The case studies discussed here are designed for the size of band one
might reasonably expect to find in school and youth organizations. This is
rather smaller than full band complement, for which a large repertoire is
published and easily available.

GENERAL PRINCIPLES

Apart from the basses, all brass band instruments are suited to melodic
work. Share out the thematic material, giving tenor instruments such as
the horn and euphonium equal importance to the cornets. Essential lines
should be clearly defined. It is preferable to double parts rather than to
attempt to write a separate line for each instrument and so clog the texture. Keep individual parts simple and within the best range of the instrument concerned. Refer to pp 60 and 151 for detailed technical information.

CASE STUDIES

Case Study 21: Carol: 'We've been awhile a-wandering'

The arrangement is designed to accompany voices; the verses are meant to
be performed by unspecified groups, with all joining in the chorus.

Instrumentation: Parts are numbered ① to ⑪ to correspond with individual band parts. This is common practice.

Parts ⑤ and ⑥ are the same, designated for baritone and euphonium,
both B♭ instruments. The parts for basses sound an octave apart, but in
view of E♭ and B♭ transpositions, both have been written into the score.

a) Minimum forces for an adequate rendering of the score: cornets 1
and 3, with baritone or euphonium and either E♭ or BB♭ bass.

b) Optional instruments: cornet 2: either baritone or euphonium: trombone: either E♭ or BB♭ bass: bass drum. The tenor horn is largely in
canon with the melody and though optional, its omission would greatly
weaken the effectiveness of the arrangement. To a lesser extent, the
same can be said of the trombone.

Key and clefs: In common with other arrangements of this carol, concert
is D minor. As this version is scored for brass band, the conventional
treble clef system has been used throughout.

Though not primarily intended to be used in this way, it does mean that in
the absence of any one B♭ instrument, another with the same transposition
can take its place. For instance, the trombone could be replaced by a
cornet, and the BB♭ bass by a euphonium. Though not advised in view of
the extensive overlapping of voices, it would even be possible for cornets
to play all the B♭ parts — six in all, and seven if the horn were to be
transposed up a fifth into B♭. The point is made only to demonstrate one
of the advantages of the treble clef system; another is that a conductor
has to be familiar with only one fingering system in order to check and
correct a wrong note for every instrument except the trombone.

With the number of performing safeguards built into the arrangement, as
already outlined, no cueing has been considered necessary in this very
short piece, during most of which everyone is in any case playing.

Time-signatures: The same procedure has been adopted as with the arrangement for orchestra.

Style and texture: the melody has been placed in the tenor range, ans-
wered in canon a bar later. In the chorus, the canon is incomplete. The
second voice, the tenor horn, having omitted the first bar of the refrain
(bar 7), takes up the canon again in bar 8 at the distance of a crotchet.
Apart from the melody and its shadow, the off-beat trio of cornets provide
rhythmic interest in the verse over the descending ostinato bass. The
trombone supplies a fifth linear strand. It has an unimportant part in

the verse, but characteristically plays a countermelody from bar 6 to the
end of the chorus, where cornets add soprano tone to reinforce the melody.

Technical points: The brass parts are not difficult, the only awkward
interval being the drop of a seventh in bar 9. The cornets will have to
place their off-beat notes very accurately in the opening bars to achieve
the desired rhythmic effect, while at the same time noting the p ⏤⏤⏤< >
p ⏤⏤⏤< > sequence.
The side-drum has possibly the trickiest part, since the player has to
alternate rapidly between compound and simple time at bar 7, and vice versa
at the 1st time bar.

FROM ORCHESTRA TO BAND
Orchestral music provides an obvious source for brass band transcriptions.
The second case study is concerned with a particular problem, that of translating accompanying string figurations into the equivalent brass language.
Another important consideration is the choice of key. A transposition into
a flat key is often required. A familiarity with instrumental counterparts
is also necessary; a guide to these follows:

Orchestral instruments		Brass band counterparts
Woodwind	flute / oboe	cornets
	clarinet	cornet/tenor horn for low passages
	bassoon	baritone, euphonium or trombone— depending on range
Brass	trumpet	cornet
	horn	tenor horn, baritone, euphonium, trombone
	trombone	trombone
	tuba	E$\flat$ and BB$\flat$ basses
Strings	violin 1	cornet 1 and repiano (tutti)
	violin 2	cornets 2 and 3

Note: low violin parts may have to be placed on tenor horn

	viola	tenor horn, baritone
	cello	baritone, euphonium
	double bass	E$\flat$ and BB$\flat$ basses

Percussion-timpani: these are not normally in a brass band, and should be
           transferred to bass drum and side drum.

Case Study 22:   Extract from 'Rosamunde' Ballet Music no 1 by Schubert

STYLE AND TEXTURE

The main problem here lies in the string writing, where smooth quaver
movement is associated with slowly shifting chords over a tonic pedal.
Just as string players have to change bows — Schubert's bass line would
need editing in this respect — brass players have to breathe. In order
to maintain the legato effect, interlocking parts are shared between two
brass instruments. Study the paired cornets, horns, trombones, and basses
in the arrangement. Always overlap parts in this manner: don't stop
before and start after the bar line.

The string quaver wiggles are quite uncharacteristic of brass writing, and
if translated literally, they would not only sound somewhat comic, but
would be very difficult to play pp, and in all probability the melody would
be smothered. Instead, quaver movement has been simulated by superimposing
the ♪♩♪♩♪ of cornets 1 and 3 over the ♩ ♩ ♩ of the horns and trombones.
The melody has been given first to cornet 2 and baritone, and then when
higher up to cornet 1 and tenor horn 1. In both cases, the octave interval, originally between clarinet and bassoon, is retained.

<u>Key</u>: Transposed down from G, most suitable for strings, to concert E♭, an
excellent key for brass band; the B♭ instruments read in F and the E♭
instruments in C. All parts lie comfortably within range.

<u>Dynamics and phrasing</u>: The whole extract is quiet. In the arrangement
the solo instruments have been marked up. The ornament in bar 7 has been
omitted from the melodic parts, being unsuited to brass. However, the
falling grace note in bar 5 should be quite easy to negotiate cleanly. It
has therefore been retained.

<u>Technical points</u>: A useful comparison can be madd between this case study
and that for brass ensemble of the beginning of the <u>Largo</u> from Dvořák's

Symphony no 9 (see pp 77-9). There the accompanying string parts are
rhythmically static, whereas here they gently move. Reference has already
been made to pairs of interlocking brass parts, which do duty for the
original strings. Notice that the euphonium is on its own and that the
continuous string pedal note has been broken into two-bar sections to
allow for breathing.

If this arrangement is to sound well, then all parts are required. It
would be possible to score for a smaller ensemble, as in the Dvořák Largo
already referred to, but in that case the material would have to be distributed differently among the instruments.

SUMMARY

The importance of choosing suitable music must be stressed — see pp 167-70
for some suggestions. Where one is arranging freely, as in the carol, the
problems are of one's own making and can be solved in the light of the
technical competence of a particular group of players. On the other hand,
where one is translating from one medium to another, as in the Schubert
extract, technical problems have to be solved in the context of what is
not only playable but also characteristic of brass scoring. In the given
case study, this applies to legato string quavers which accompany a simple
melody. The other problem which this piece highlights is that compared
with woodwind and strings, the overall tessitura of the brass family is
low, especially at a junior level. Trumpet and cornet players cannot be
expected to play in the same pitch area as upper strings and woodwind.
Bars 7-8 need good lip and breath control to sound musical at the dynamic
level indicated. Unlike the orchestra, the brass band is particularly
rich in solo instruments in the tenor range, the euphonium being the most
obvious example. The verse section of the carol arrangement provides evi-
dence of a melody placed in the middle of the score.

As with all arranging, try to think in terms of tone colour. Brass instruments are generally homogeneous in this respect, but they do have individuality and this must be exploited, as in the case of the tenor range instruments referred to above.

Chapter XI
Arranging for concert wind band

Deriving from the military band, the concert (or symphonic) wind band is now firmly established. It has gradually been seen to be worthy of serious attention, and leading twentieth-century composers, including Holst, Vaughan Williams, and Copland, have contributed to a rapidly growing repertoire.

GENERAL PRINCIPLES

<u>Instrumentation</u>: There is no generally accepted constitution. A big band might include clarinets and saxophones of all known sizes and with such forces, arranging is a highly professional skill. However, we are here concerned with the instruments more usually found in typical military and junior concert bands. These are listed on pp 138-9. The most useful and versatile instrument is the clarinet, with its wide range and tonal flexibility. The clarinet section is to the concert wind band what the violins and viola are to the full orchestra, and it is to the advantage of the many players of this popular instrument that so many can be usefully employed within the band.

At the technical level in which we are interested, there is not much scope for complex or idiomatic scoring. Any arrangement must aim to be musically effective while involving the majority of players in interesting if simple material.

<u>Texture and blend</u>: Inevitably, there will be much doubling of voices in tutti passages, since it is unwise to write in more than four or five real parts. It is important to give sufficient tonal weight to the main melody and the bass-line. The relative weakness in number and tone of the lower woodwind compared with the strength of the lower brass should be noted. Equally, the upper woodwind are individually more varied in timbre and can play higher than cornets and trumpets which, if scored in unison, can nevertheless outmatch the woodwind in intensity of sound. But remember that ten crying babies do not sound louder than one really miserable infant. A single high-pitched screamer can always be heard above the rest. In the same way, one piccolo will add more point to a melody line than the addition of extra cornets.

CASE STUDIES

Two types of arrangement have been selected: the first a free working of the carol in a utility version, the second an expansion of part of Byrd's variations on 'The Carman's Whistle', first referred to on p 3. Here the scoring is more individually conceived, safety-first cover being provided by cross-cueing rather than by doubling every line.

Carol: 'We've been awhile a-wandering'

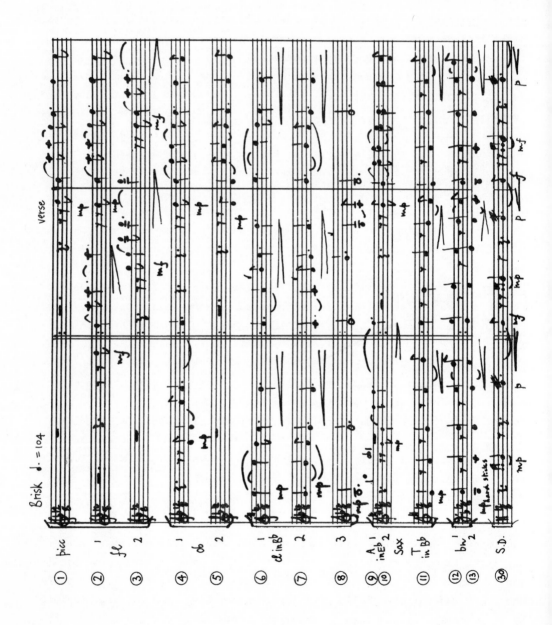

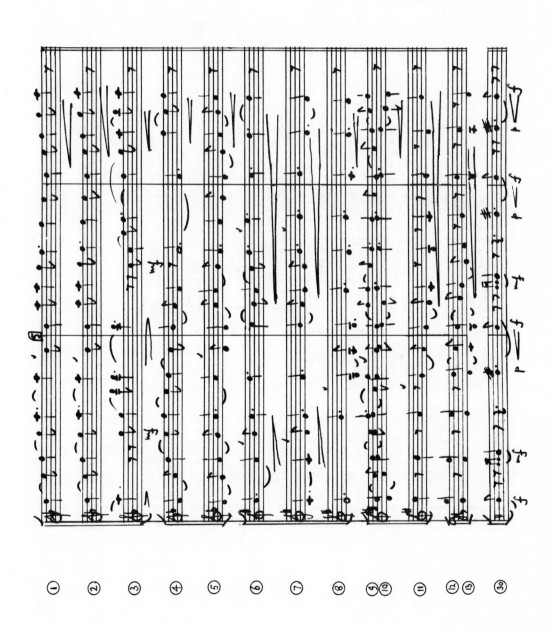

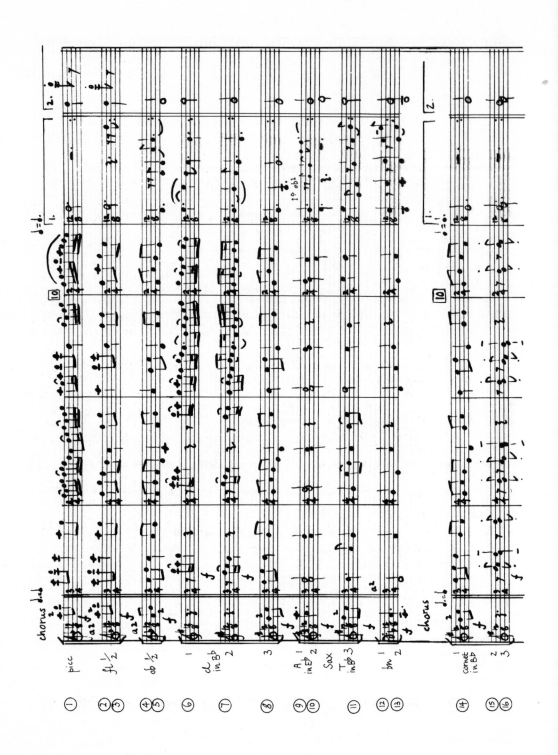

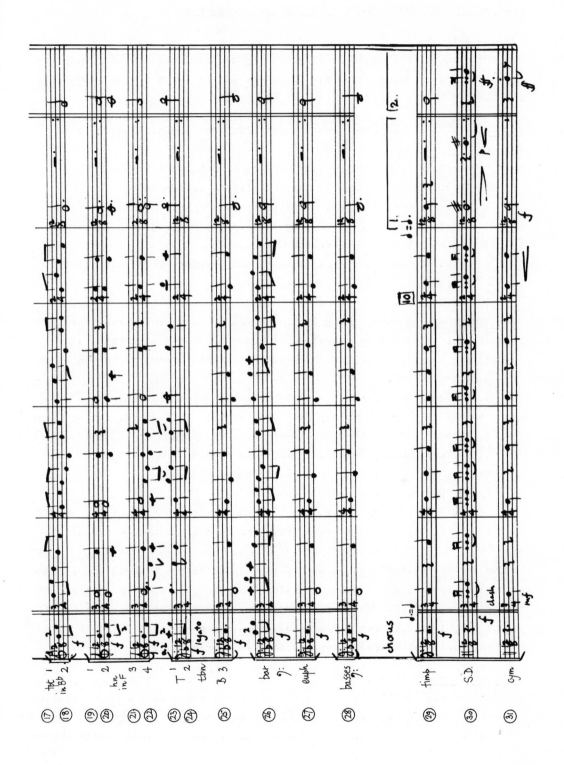

Case Study 23: Carol 'We've been awhile a-wandering'

GENERAL PRINCIPLES
The verse is set for woodwind only and the chorus for either the whole band
or woodwind only or brass only. The piece can be performed by relatively
few players, as detailed in the analysis on the next page.

Texture: With a full complement of players, the layout of parts is as
follows:
bars 1-4: melody in piccolo, flute 1, oboe 2, and alto saxophone 1.
          ostinato bass line in tenor saxophone and bassoons.
          ostinato filler parts in clarinets, playing in three parts.
          filler part, rhythmically following the melody in 6ths or 3rds,
          oboe 1 and alto saxophone 2 in octaves.
          flute 2 adds a figure based on the opening 5th of the melody.
          side-drum has a rhythmic ostinato.
     The melody is heard over three octaves, the bass line over two.
     Though the texture may appear to be complex from the above description,
     it is in fact fairly transparent; only the melody and its shadow
     move to any great extent. The ostinato parts are based on scales in
     contrary motion.
bars 5-6: modulation to F major: the ostinato patterns collapse.
bar 7 to end of chorus: melody over four octaves in piccolo, flutes 1 and
     2, oboes 1 and 2, clarinet 3, cornet 1, trumpets 1 and 2, and baritone.
     Bass line: unison bassoons 1 and 2, euphonium, bass trombone, and
     basses.
     Filler parts: 1) clarinets 1 and 2
                   2) alto saxophones 1 and 2, much as horns 1, 2, and 3
                   3) tenor saxophone, horn 4, and baritone — a counter-
                      melodic part.
Notice the elaborated version of the tune given to the piccolo, an instrument which characteristically decorates the melody in tutti passages. In
this arrangement, designed for accompanying community singing, the melody
of the chorus is very heavily scored, both in the number of type of instruments designated and by the spread over four octaves.

Instrumentation: In a score using so many different instruments, there is
bound to be much doubling. Since this is a utility arrangement, suited to
a variety of performing conditions, it is necessary to identify the instruments allotted to each essential musical line. One can then decide which

instruments are dispensable in the event of reduced forces. Preferred
instruments are listed first, alternatives in brackets.

Verse woodwind	Chorus woodwind	Chorus brass
S^1:(melody): fl 1 (ob 2, picc, a.sax 1)	fl 1 (fl 2, ob 1, ob 2, picc, cl 3)	S :(melody): cornet 1 (tpt 1, tpt 2, bar)
S^2: ob 1 (a.sax 2)	cl 1 and 2	A^1: cornets 2 and 3
A : cl 1 and 2	a.sax 1 and 2	A^2: hn 1 and 2 (hn 3)
T : cl 3	t.sax	T : t.tbn 1 (t.tbn 2, hn 4)
B : bn 2 (t.sax, bn 1)	bn 2 (bn 1)	B : basses (b.tbn, euph)

Note: fl 2 provides optional descant

Minimum forces: first choice WOODWIND: fl 1: cl 1,2,3: a.sax 1,2: t.sax:
(whole piece)   bn 2. The tenor saxophone, with only an added part in the
                    chorus, can be omitted.

Minimum forces: first choice BRASS: cornets 1,2,3: t.tbn 1: $E^\flat$ bass.
(chorus only)   Filler parts for hns 1 and 2 are not essential.

Percussion: the side-drum is ad lib, but its part adds much to the
                    arrangement. The timpani can be omitted.

From the above tables, it will be seen that the piece can be performed by
relatively few players.

Cued parts: with so much doubling, only the introductory entry of oboe 1
has been cued through to alto saxophone 1, one of the essential instruments.

Clefs: for the concert wind band, it is usual to write in the bass clef
for the lower brass. If necessary, individual band parts can be transposed
for players familiar only with the brass band treble clef system. Similarly, if only tenor horns are available, band parts will have to be written
up a tone. Woodwind transpositions are normal.

Key: as in other versions of this carol, D minor/F major has been retained,
a key very suited to wind in general.

Style: Reference has already been made to the ostinato figures, the scoring
of the melody, bass line and filler parts, and to the texture in general.
A few detailed points can be added. In the chorus, notice that the woodwind are more active than the characteristically less agile brass. Joining
the piccolo in flourishes are the two top clarinets. While they can play
in semiquavers, cornets 2 and 3, also punctuating the melody with off-beat
interjections, have suitably simpler parts.

As in the orchestral version of this carol (see pp 114-5) the pair of timpani have to compromise on suitable notes in a passage which modulates from F major to D minor. Chords of C, F and A are served by C; B$\flat$, G minor, and D minor by D.

The side-drum has the most telling part with an ostinato rhythmic pattern in the verse in which the crescendo roll at the end of each bar motivates the marching tread of the piece, suggested by the words of the carollers.

SUMMARY

In this arrangement, every effort has been made to give essential material to those instruments most likely to be found in school and youth bands. For example, supposing there is no tenor saxophone player available, then his part in the chorus can be taken by the more commonly owned trombone. In the verse, a lack of bass woodwind instruments can be rectified by handing the absent bassoon players' parts to any or all of baritone, euphonium, and bass trombone players. The price to be paid for compromise of this kind is that part-writing must be kept simple, with an eye and ear to multiple use.

The next case study will use the instruments of a reduced concert wind band in a more individual and idiomatic way.

Case Study 24: 'The Carman's Whistle' by William Byrd (from The Fitzwilliam
Virginal Book, no 58)

<u>Case Study 24: 'The Carman's Whistle' by William Byrd</u>

GENERAL PRINCIPLES

This arrangement presents the theme, obviously popular in origin, and two
variations out of a total of eight in Byrd's keyboard piece. Bars 23-34
form the finale of the set.

Technical demands are greater than in the previous case study. The scoring
is for small wind band, and both woodwind and brass are essential to performance.

<u>Texture</u>: Byrd's original part-writing has been retained almost throughout;
unison and octave doublings are used extensively to strengthen important
melodic lines. The treatment of the bass line in the tutti sections in
bars 5-8 and 13-16 should allow for a less heavy emphasis on main beats.
The texture in bars 17-28 (Variation 6) is reduced in conformity with
Byrd's original where, in comparison with the final section, thick left-
hand chords are the exception rather than the rule. In this last section,
Byrd writes in up to six parts, reflected in the tutti scoring of the first
and last four bars.

<u>Instrumentation</u>: The following instruments, all cross-cued where playing
an essential part, are optional:

    clarinet 3, alto and tenor saxophones, bassoon, cornet 3, horn 2,
    trombone 2, and baritone.

<u>Key</u>: down a tone into B$^\flat$, a most convenient key for the many transposing
instruments.

<u>Style</u>: Byrd's original keyboard version is full of the standard ornament
signs — ⸙ and ⸙ . The exact interpretation of these is open to some con-
jecture, and being generally unsuited to woodwind and brass, they have
been omitted, with the exception of the written out sextuplets in bars 30
and 34. These happen to lie conveniently under the fingers of flautists
and oboists.

An attempt has been made to vary the timbre and pitch levels, particularly
in bars 17-28, where reduced forces of woodwind are contrasted first with
brass trio, then with a mixed group of saxophones, bassoon, and horn 1,
and finally with flute, piccolo, and three clarinets. All dynamics are
editorial.

SUMMARY

When writing for concert wind band, the following points deserve consideration:

a) Much orchestral music can be adapted and used as source material. In a full wind band, the upper woodwind are capable of matching the agility of violins and this means that a wider repertoire can be considered compared with the limitations imposed by the brass band — the narrow pitch range, uniform tone colour, and the technical problems to be overcome in playing fast-moving music at a junior level of competence.

b) The choice of a suitable key is essential. As the transposing instruments concerned are in B^b, F and E^b, it follows that flat keys are most appropriate. Non-transposing woodwind have to get used to playing in up to three flats, and the lower brass parts in a concert wind band, even if written at concert pitch in the bass clef, are still related to instruments built in B^b and E^b, and therefore can use open notes and simple fingerings to produce good tone and intonation.

c) Think in terms of timbre. Exploit the variety of colour between individual members of the woodwind and between woodwind and brass choirs. Remember that, as in the orchestra, horns blend well with bassoons and clarinets. Contrast groups of high woodwind with the low brass. Vary the texture — one instrument to a part alternating with heavy unison and octave doublings of important elements.

d) Use percussion to add spice and point, but remember that it is the more effective if reserved for the appropriate occasion — for a crescendo, a climax, or for special effects.

Part 3 Chapter XII
Reference Transposition

For reasons that are largely historical, a number of instruments, mostly members of the brass band family, are so-called transposing instruments. Players, conductors, composers, and arrangers must know that:

WRITTEN pitch / notes = the transposed part as written in the score and in the player's part

CONCERT pitch / notes = the part as it sounds, and as written for untransposed instruments

A piano tuned to concert pitch therefore sounds as it is written: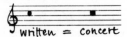

If a piano were to be tuned down a tone, it would become a transposing instrument, a piano 'in B♭'. When designating any transposing instrument, the relationship of the concert note is always made to the written note C:

Therefore to sound concert C, music for the 'B♭' piano would have to be transposed up a tone, becoming, in this case, D:

In the above and all subsequent examples, the concert note will be shown as a square note.

Nearly all transposing instruments sound lower than written. The common exceptions are: descant recorder, piccolo, and a number of small tuned percussion — soprano xylophone and glockenspiel and all chime bars. These all sound an octave higher than written.

With a capo the guitar effectively becomes an upward transposing instrument; the interval depends on the position of the capo (see p 88). If placed behind the second fret, it will be a guitar 'in D', where written C sounds D. At the same time, the guitar is a downward transposing instrument, being written in the treble clef and sounding down an octave.

The transposing instruments most likely to be encountered are listed below in alphabetical order. The first note given is that which must be written to sound middle C, where this is possible. School tuned percussion will be listed as a group on their own at the end.

Instruments marked * are particularly associated with treble clef brass band conventions - see Chapters IV and X.

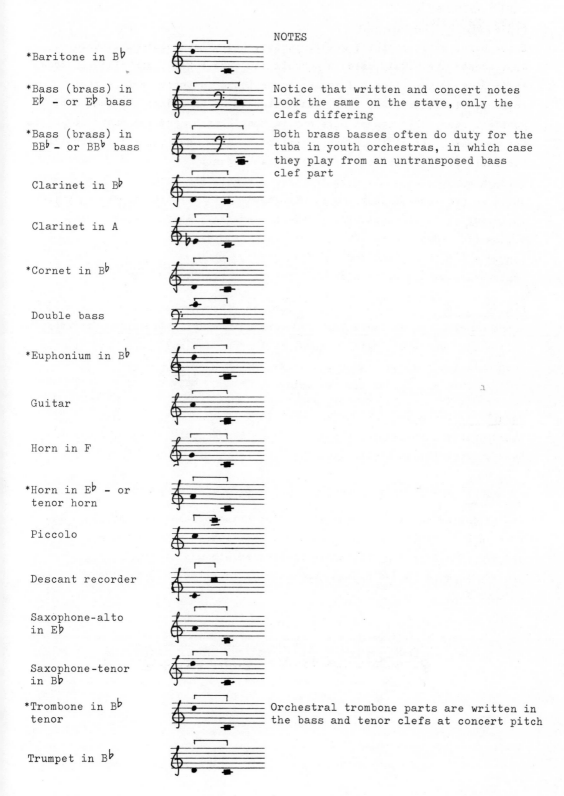

NOTES

*Baritone in B♭

*Bass (brass) in
E♭ - or E♭ bass

Notice that written and concert notes
look the same on the stave, only the
clefs differing

*Bass (brass) in
BB♭ - or BB♭ bass

Both brass basses often do duty for the
tuba in youth orchestras, in which case
they play from an untransposed bass
clef part

Clarinet in B♭

Clarinet in A

*Cornet in B♭

Double bass

*Euphonium in B♭

Guitar

Horn in F

*Horn in E♭ - or
tenor horn

Piccolo

Descant recorder

Saxophone-alto
in E♭

Saxophone-tenor
in B♭

*Trombone in B♭
tenor

Orchestral trombone parts are written in
the bass and tenor clefs at concert pitch

Trumpet in B♭

TUNED PERCUSSION

Chime bars, glockenspiels, metallophones, and xylophones —all these
instruments are widely used in schools and have taken their place in group
music of many varieties. They are to be found in three basic sizes:
soprano, alto/tenor, and bass, but design is as varied as the number of
manufacturers. The lowest note may be C or F or G, and the range upward is
not standard. It is therefore important to know what sort of instrument is
available to avoid writing an impracticable part.

Parts are normally written in the treble clef; the range is restricted by
the size and type of instrument. To simplify the reading of parts by young
children, it is suggested that these are written, as far as possible,
within the stave, as is the case with the recorder family.

Assume a set of soprano and alto/tenor
instruments with a written range:

Concert pitch will be as follows: soprano glockenspiel — two octaves up:
soprano metallophone and xylophone — one octave up: alto/tenor glockenspiel — one octave up: alto/tenor metallophone and xylophone — as written.
Bass metallophone and xylophone, best written:
will in this case sound down an octave.

Tunable tambours and tambourines come in various sizes, and each can be
tuned over an interval of about a fifth. For school purposes, parts are
best written in the treble .clef.

PRACTICAL EFFECTS OF TRANSPOSITION ON SCORING FOR INSTRUMENTS

In the following examples the effects of transposition on a simple hymn
tune in D major (concert) are shown in relation to wind instruments in B♭
and E♭. The key, very suited to elementary strings, is not sympathetic to
the wind. Here is the opening of Handel's tune for the hymn 'Rejoice, the
Lord is King':

Transposed for clarinet and trumpet in B♭ and tenor horn in E♭, we find
the following:

Comment: add two sharps to key-signature. Clarinet lies uncomfortably
           over the 'break' in bars 1-2.

Comment: add three sharps to key-signature. Part lies rather high.
           Taking it down an octave, it is on the low side.

Conversely, putting the brass into their easiest keys can make difficulties
for elementary strings. Here the brass are comfortable, but a cellist,
though playing in first position, would have to manage forward and backward
extensions across the top two strings. These generally lead to insecure
intonation.

A quick rule-of-thumb: when writing for transposing instruments, the
following sharps and flats must be added to or subtracted from the key-
signature of the written part:

        for transposing instruments in F : plus 1 sharp or less 1 flat
        for transposing instruments in B♭: plus 2 sharps or less 2 flats
        for transposing instruments in E♭: plus 3 sharps or less 3 flats

Writing music

GENERAL PRINCIPLES

Conventional musical notation is a communication system by which a complex-
ity of signs represent sounds. To the performer these signs should indicate
not only the pitch and duration of notes, but how the notes should sound in
terms of loudness, quality, and expression. To present this information
clearly is the prime aim of the notator. The following discussion points
are not intended as a comprehensive survey of notation. They are confined
to a few tips on the physical act of writing and to features of notation un-
familiar to those whose experience has been concerned mainly with keyboard
music.

MUSICAL CALLIGRAPHY

Clarity and legibility are all-important.

Writing implements: For bar lines and written instructions, a ball-point
pen is clear and less messy to use than a nib pen. For the music itself,
use a nib pen. Notation demands thick and thin, heavy and light strokes.

Corrections: When writing in ink or biro, cover a mistake with pre-gummed
strip or an off-cut of staved paper. Any attempt to erase by scraping will
break the surface of the paper, and corrections will then become hazardous.
Two methods of affixing off-cuts are recommended. Normal gluing is messy,
but modern spray mount adhesives are very effective, if expensive. The
second method is to use Scotch Magic Tape, a type of Sellotape, which
'takes' biro or soft pencil, does not tarnish or harden, and can be photo-
copied without reflecting light. With very minor mistakes, 'typing error'
paper or a correction pen will help cover up the odd wrong note or dot.
Amendments can then be made in biro or soft pencil. Ordinary ink is not
suitable for this; only drawing ink (Indian or Chinese) should be used.

Heads and tails: Relate the size of note-heads to that of the stave:

Note heads are made by a short heavy stroke with the broadest face of the
nib or by drawing a very small circle or twirl or two close crescents, with
no window in the centre. Opening out the crescents will give a minim. Similar effects can be achieved by the skilful use of a nylon tip pen:

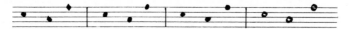

Tails or stems: if there is one part to a stave, draw tails below notes
above the middle line and above notes below the middle line. Notes on the
middle line have tails going either way, following the majority of notes
within the bar:

This also applies to quavers joined by a crook.
Where there are two parts to a stave, the top
has tails up and the bottom tails down:

<u>Leger-lines</u> should be spaced to scale:
<u>Quavers and Crooks</u>
Avoid drawing a crook along a stave line:
If the overall movement is up, the crook
should slope up in sympathy. Tails are
thin, crooks thick:

SOME NOTATIONAL CONVENTIONS

Rests

Avoid the obsolete crotchet rest (𝄽), which can be confused with other symbols. A consistent manuscript version of the crotchet rest is more important than an exact imitation of its printed form: ᛉ for 𝄽   A whole
bar rest, whatever the time-signature, is always:

Bar repetition signs

These are best avoided. They can confuse the player who should be looking
forward, not backward.
Rather than:

write:

Writing at pitch

With the exception of some contemporary music, scores and parts are at
'written' pitch (see pp 150-4). Where very high parts cannot be accommodated between the staves of a score, write the part down an octave, pre-
faced by 8^{ve}. The player, however, relates visual symbols to physical
actions rather than to named sounding notes. For example, the flautist's
embouchure and fingering are different for phrases which here appear an
octave apart, but which are in fact identical:

To help the player, write: rather than:

WRITTEN INSTRUCTIONS

<u>Tempo</u> indications, whether at the beginning or during a piece, are written
above the score and, in the case of a full orchestra, a second time above
the string section.

<u>Expression</u> marks are written below each part. Slurs, staccato dots, and
other such marks are placed on the
opposite side from the stem of a
note:

Only when two parts are written on
a single stave are they on the same
side as the stems, which can be confusing and is a good reason for in-
sisting on writing only one part to
a stave. Notice also how adjacent
staves are infringed:

<u>Bar numbers</u> should be inserted at the top of the score. Depending on the
length of the piece and the number of bars to a page, every ⑤ or ⑩ will
suffice, but ensure that there is at least one number on each page. Number
the beginning of each bar concerned and ignore an up-beat or incomplete bar
at the start of a piece. Take care with 1st and 2nd time bars, where [15a]
and [15b] are preferred to consecutive numbering. Band parts must be
numbered identically with the score.

THE SCORE

<u>Order of instruments</u>

For the ordering of instruments within a system and systems within a score,
refer to examples and case studies. Horns and the piano require special
consideration.

In the traditional orchestral score horns are placed above trumpets. This
is because in the early Classical orchestra horns usually associated with
the woodwind lying above, while trumpets were linked to drums, lying immediately below — trombones had not yet found a regular place in the orchestra. There is little logic in retaining this convention and it is suggested that the order commonly found in the brass ensemble should be adopted
for the orchestral score, with trumpets at the top of the system.

A piano part included to provide ad lib basic harmonic support is best
placed at the bottom of the score. If it is integral to the work, as in
Stravinsky's <u>Petrushka</u>, it is placed immediately above the string section.

<u>Planning the layout of a score on the page</u>

Legibility is essential to the score-reader. Consider the following points
when planning the layout — they will help to achieve visual clarity. Spare
staves are wasted at the bottom of the page — use them as spacers between
each system. This visually separates the instrumental groups and allows
one to write in dynamic marks and other information. It is better to have
too many than too few staves.

Imagine scoring for a standard 'small' orchestra:

Woodwind:	fl 1 (fl 2), ob, cl 1, cl 2, bn	6 staves	
spacer		1 stave	
Brass:	tpt 1, tpt 2, hn, tbn	4 staves	
spacer		1 stave	total
Percussion:	timps + one other	2 staves	20
spacer		1 stave	staves
Strings:	vn 1, vn 2, va (or vn 3), vc, db	5 staves	

22-stave paper will suffice: 24-stave paper will allow adequate extra
space for a piano rehearsal score, should this be required.

Staves

The staves of each family or group are bracketed together to form
a system. Where there are two or more instruments of the same
kind, such as violins or clarinets, they are braced
together.

Using one stave for a pair of instruments is sometimes possible (see pp 114, 128, and 136), but
crossing parts can be confusing to read:

Similarly, the crooks of paired instruments
become interlaced and leave no room for the
addition of phrase marks:

This applies most particularly to clarinets,
whose wide range can leave the stave itself
empty:

The double bass, which at a junior level often has a simplified version of
the cello part, should also be given its own stave. Ideally, therefore,
each instrument should have a separate stave.

Bars

The number of bars to a page will depend on many factors — time-signature,
tempo, the incidence of notes of small value, and, if there is a vocal
part, the space required to underlay the text.

Musical rhythms are more easily read if bars are of equal length. For
example, standard 12-stave paper has staves 19 cm long. If 6 bars can be
accommodated with comfort, divide the stave as follows, giving the first
bar an extra cm to allow for clef, key, and time signatures:

Bar lines

To emphasize the visual break between instrumental groups, draw bar lines
down through each system but not between systems; refer to any full score.
A rectangular blockboard, about 50 cm by 40 cm, marked out as shown below,
will greatly facilitate the rapid drawing of vertical and accurately
spaced bar lines. At the bottom of the board, mark off the various numbers of bars which fit different sizes of manuscript paper: 24-stave
scoring paper is wider than the figures quoted above for 12-stave paper.
Line up the staves with the left hand margin and, using a T-square, bar out
a whole page at a time:

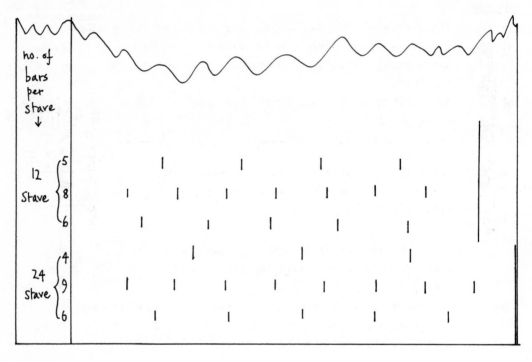

Spacing within the bar

Within a bar, space note values in accordance with their visual length:

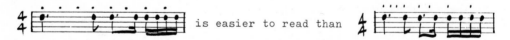

is easier to read than

In a score, make sure that notes line up vertically:

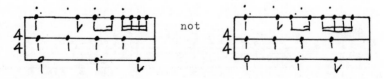

not

BAND PARTS

The needs of the performer are the prime consideration in notating instrumental parts, generally termed 'band' parts. The hints that follow will
help the copyist provide the minimum information in a clear and legible
manner.

a) The player sees his part from a distance, often in indifferent light.
   Make sure that parts are written boldly in dense ink or with a felt pen.
   Use large-scale 12-stave paper.

b) Small pieces of paper tend to fall or be blown off a music stand.
   Resist the temptation to economize by writing parts on narrow strips of
   paper cut out of a sheet.

c) Avoid awkward turns. At the cost of wasting a stave, arrange for a
   turn during a rest.

d) Insert bar numbers or letters as in the full score

e) Long rests:  not

   An essential bar number or letter must be inserted in a long rest:

    not

   After a long rest, cue in a prominent part for a bar or two as a check
   to accurate counting. It does wonders for the player's confidence:

f) Write out repeated bars in full, numbering the bars above:

g) All dynamics, bowing, tonguing and written instructions must be inserted
   into every part.

h) Transposing and treble clef band parts must be written in the appropriate transposed key, whatever conventions are used in the full score.

i) Where a part lies
   well above the
   stave, as with the      not
   flute, write on
   alternate staves:

j) Cued in or alternative parts must be clearly marked and written in a
   smaller face:

k) Write only one part on a sheet. For those who sit askew, especially
   wind players, sharing a stand makes it difficult to keep music and conductor in line with the eye. Furthermore, writing a pair of wind parts
   on a single sheet is often a false economy. It takes longer as the
   parts have to be braced on a pair of staves, and further problems are
   mentioned on pp 156-7 above. Paper is wasted and turns are difficult.
   Only two players can use the part and if, as is often the case with
   clarinets and trumpets, parts are doubled, then a second copy is anyway
   necessary. Separate cl 1 and cl 2 parts will also service a total of
   four players.

SUMMARY

One pleads for a bold, strong hand, accurate in detail, and visually well-
proportioned. Some composers have notoriously poor musical handwriting
while others, such as Henry Purcell, invariably make their scores as
pleasing to the eye as they are to the ear.

Opening of the
'Golden' Sonata
by Henry Purcell.
(Reproduced by
permission of the
British Library Board.)

Copying music

Modern methods of copying manuscript music vary in quality, efficiency and expense. The following information is provided for those who want to prepare scores and parts for reproduction on machines generally found in schools and similar institutions, or by using local firms which offer copying facilities.

METHODS OF REPRODUCTION

<u>PHOTOCOPYING</u> (eg Rank Xerox, 3M)

Not the cheapest method, but one of the easiest to use. A well-adjusted machine will reproduce accurately from soft pencil, biro or ink. Gradations of shading, heavy and light strokes — these will all be faithfully reproduced — an important factor in the presentation of manuscript music. Where only a few copies are required, this method is certainly the best and quickest.

Where large numbers are required, it is possible to combine photocopying with either spirit or stencil duplicating.

<u>Reduction</u>: this will be discussed more fully on p 164. At this point it is sufficient to mention that photocopying machines now exist which will reduce an original to a size (A4) which can then be used for further copying on a standard machine.

<u>Quantities</u>: it is course possible to run off a number of copies on a photocopying machine fitted with this capability. In this case, the first few copies, usually up to 6, are rather expensive. Thereafter the price is very competitive with other methods.

<u>SPIRIT DUPLICATING</u> (eg Banda, Offrex)

All schools have machines of this type and the method provides a cheap and simple way of copying music, provided that the following points are kept in mind:

<u>Definition</u>: this is rather poor and in effect it means that the size of type associated with a typewriter is about the smallest symbol which can be effectively copied. Edges tend to be blurred, and for clarity it is therefore important that musical symbols are large in scale. This method is usually satisfactory for individual band and voice parts, and it is possible to run off about 100 copies from one transfer sheet.

<u>Transfer sheets</u>, pre-lined with staves, can be obtained. However, with these one is restricted to the spacing provided between staves, which is somewhat limited if many verbal instructions and dynamics have to be inserted.

Alternatively, staves can be ruled with a special wheeled scriber, also
suitable for stencil skins, but this is laborious, and mistakes can only be
crossed out, not erased.

Copy paper: single- and double-sided paper is available, the latter having
the disadvantage that turns are generally to be avoided in band parts. In
any case, copy paper is rather flimsy, thin and therefore translucent. As
most parts can be accommodated on two single sheets, it is usually best to
tape these together, thus providing some rigidity and avoiding the necessity for turns.

Summary: a cheap and effective method of duplicating individual instrumental
parts where large quantities are required.

HEAT SPIRIT DUPLICATING

This involves making a spirit master transfer sheet from an original manuscript by the 'heat transfer' method, thus avoiding the need to write
directly onto a transfer sheet. For this it is first necessary to photo-
copy the original, using a machine which prints with an element of carbon.
Both photocopying and the production of a spirit master can be carried out
on a machine such as the 3M model 45. Thereafter the process is completed
on a normal spirit duplicator. The same constraints apply to the suitability of material to be copied as have been mentioned above.

STENCIL DUPLICATING (Roneo, Gestetner etc)

Stencil copying machines are found in most educational establishments.
They can be used in two ways:

a) by 'engraving' a waxed sheet with a style. It is important to use a
   stencil designed for the purpose, having a softer surface than found on
   a typing stencil. Staves can be incised with the special wheeled
   scriber mentioned above. To cut a stencil is a laborious process, and
   mistakes have to be erased by painting over with a form of shellac (or
   nail varnish), through which one can make a new incision. From a well-
   cut stencil, an unlimited number of copies can be made. These will be
   clear and well defined, to a standard which is not matched by the spirit
   duplicating method.

b) By using a photocopier, printing with an element of carbon, in conjunction with a stencil copier. As with heat spirit duplicating, both
   processes are combined in the 3M model 45. This avoids the labour and
   shortcomings of cutting a stencil by hand. Copies are run off in the
   usual way. Definition is good, and it is possible to produce copies of
   which the original has been reduced.

DYELINE

This method is only suitable where a considerable number of copies are
required of the score or, for instance, chorus parts of a large-scale work.
As with any method, there are advantages and disadvantages: these will become apparent in discussing the following points:

a) Dyeline copying machines are located in surveyors', architects', and
   engineers' offices. Commercial firms also undertake copying work for
   these professions, and most towns support such a 'copy shop'. Before
   starting a large-scale project involving this method of duplicating, a
   visit to the nearest office or shop will establish what size of copy
   paper is available.

b) Copy paper: the normal machine will accommodate a roll of paper 76 cm
   wide. Length, for practical purposes, is unlimited.

c) A form of translucent tracing paper must be used for the original.
   This can be obtained, pre-lined with 12, 18, or more staves, from a
   good music shop. Notation should be in black ink (Indian ink is not
   essential) which, when used in a broad-nibbed fountain pen, will give a
   very adequate result. Verbal instructions and bar lines are best
   written with a black biro or a Rotring pen.

d) Errors: these may be corrected in the following ways:
   1) a small error can be scraped away with a very sharp blade. Write
      in the correction in biro or soft lead pencil: ink will run, as
      the surface of the paper will have been broken by the scraping.
   2) a large error is best corrected by cutting out a section of the
      paper and sticking a new piece into the gap. Use 3M Scotch Magic
      Transparent Tape, which will not reflect light in the copying
      process, and over which it is possible to write in biro or pencil.
      Note that errors cannot be covered over with opaque paper, as this
      will print as a black patch in the final copy.

e) Preparation for the printer: tape the pages of the score in a double
   row, using the same brand tape as mentioned above:

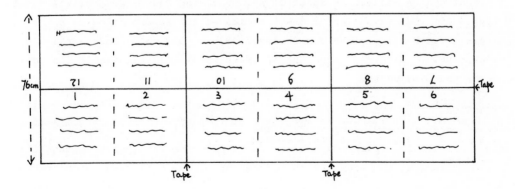

The diagram represents a 12-page score — there is of course no limit to
the number of pages possible. The printed copy will emerge from the
machine as a single sheet of paper, and will be costed by the metre.
By using the full width of the copy paper in the manner described, waste
is avoided and an economical way of printing is the result.

f) Folding: it is unnecessary to bind the copy. First fold along the
centre spine, printed matter to the outside. Then pleat the pages as
shown below. To avoid confusion over pagination, number the pages in
the middle, not at left or right hand sides.

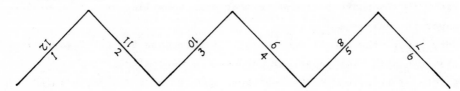

If necessary, trim the bottom edge, and staple the loose ends. No
further binding is necessary. The incredulous are invited to fold a
piece of paper as outlined above. Open at page 1 and continue turning
until page 12 is reached.

Summary

The preparation of the original for the dyeline method is fairly laborious.
However, it produces a very acceptable copy at a reasonable price and
avoids the cost of binding. The original can be rolled up, will last for
ever and can be used again and again for further copies, should they be
required.

PAPER SIZES

When planning the layout of scores or parts for copying it is essential to
consider the standard sizes of paper which are available for use with
duplicating machines.

Standard 12-stave manuscript paper is wider than either foolscap or quarto
paper sizes, which are being phased out with the general adoption of the
international A module. A sheet of A4, measuring 210 by 297 mm, will just
accommodate the stave area of 12-stave manuscript paper, allowing a narrow
margin at each side. American foolscap, 215 by 330 mm, allows a slightly
wider margin. Either of these paper sizes is therefore suitable for small
scores and band parts.

REDUCTION

Large scores, requiring up to 24-stave paper, will not fit standard paper
sizes as used in copying machines. Short of using the dyeline method for
reproduction, it is necessary to reduce manuscript originals before making

photocopies. Provided one keeps within A3 size, 297 by 420 mm, which will
comfortably accommodate a 24-stave sheet measuring 270 by 400 mm, then
access to a machine such as the Xerox 7000 photocopier will enable reduction, graded in five degrees. For example, A3 will reduce to A4 — half
size — by applying the third degree of reduction. The resulting copy is
very clear and well-defined.

The reduction of a large manuscript will always produce a clearer result
than any that can be achieved by writing the original 'in miniature'. The
typescript and music examples in this book have been reduced to two-thirds
of the size of the original copy.

CONCLUSION

It will be appreciated that different problems require different solutions
and that there is no one answer to the particular problem of copying
scores and parts. The foregoing suggestions outline some of the more
obvious possibilities. One that has not been sufficiently tested is the
projection onto a screen, by overhead projector, of transparencies made
from original manuscripts by a thermal photocopier with this facility,
such as the 3M model 45. Since the music would have to remain in score,
the method would only be suitable where a limited number of instruments
are involved.

Bibliography

This is not intended as a comprehensive list of books covering all aspects
of a complicated subject; it simply points the way to further reading on
problems related to writing and arranging music.

Baines, Anthony: Woodwind Instruments and their History,
                 (Faber) London   1957
        A most valuable account of aspects of technique, style, and
        history. A mine of information.
Boustead, Alan: Writing down Music   (OUP) London 1975
        Full treatment of the subject.
Cole, Hugo: Sounds and Signs   (OUP) London 1974
        Stimulating thought on notation.
Forsyth, Cecil: Orchestration (Macmillan) London 1914 (revised 2nd edition
                 1935)
        This remains a classic and is invaluable.
Lang, Philip J.: Scoring for the Band (Mills Music) New York 1950
        Covers concert wind, military, and marching bands.
Lawrence, Ian: Brass in Your School (OUP) London 1975
        Useful more for its extensive repertoire list than for information
        suggested by its title.
Piston, Walter: Orchestration (Gollancz) London 1955
        The best of the more recent books on the subject.
Wagner, Joseph: Band Scoring (McGraw-Hill) New York 1960
        Expensive, comprehensive.
Wagner, Joseph: Orchestration (McGraw-Hill) New York 1959
        Expensive, comprehensive; particularly good on translation of
        keyboard figuration.
Wood, Alexander: The Physics of Music (Methuen) London 1944
        In spite of its age, this is still an invaluable book, and does
        relate science to music.
Wright, Denis: Scoring for Brass Band (Baker) London 1967
        The best short book on the subject.

Source list of music

The following list of music will provide suitable material for arrangements at all levels of difficulty. It is important to remember, however, that a composer's music is copyright until fifty years after his death, and it is an offence to make arrangements of copyright music — even if only for use in one's own school, youth orchestra, or band — without first obtaining the publisher's permission.

Of necessity, this list must be selective. After a general section giving the sort of material which can be adapted for all types of instrumental groups, separate entries concentrate on the genres of music which suit the particular forces discussed in Chapters II - XI.

GENERAL

Community songs, carols and hymns

The number of publications precludes detailed listing.

Folk songs and dances

The Penguin Book of English Folk Songs, ed R. Vaughan Williams and A. L. Lloyd (Penguin) London 1959

The English Folk Dance and Song Society publish numerous collections, such as:

The Country Dance Book and Country Dance Tunes, ed Cecil Sharp (Novello) London 1909-22

The Ballad Literature and Popular Music of Olden Time, by William Chappell, 2 vols (Dover - reprint) New York 1965

Dover have also published a number of collections of American folk songs.

Renaissance consort music

Much of the repertoire has been arranged for recorders, and the following list is anything but comprehensive. Entries under publishers; catalogue numbers in brackets:

Heugel

Le Pupitre series

Attaingnant, Pierre: Danseries a 4 parties (1547) (LP 9). Perhaps the best edition of this collection. In score.

London Pro Musica Edition: a useful series of consort music, including:

Gervaise, Claude: Cinquiesme livre de danceries (1550) a 4 (AD 5)

Moeck

Der Bläserchor series: suitable not only for wind instruments, this collection concentrates on music in which the individual parts have a very restricted range. In score:

Attaingnant, Pierre: Second livre de danceries (1547) a 4 (3603)

Attaingnant, Pierre: Quart et Cinquiesme livres de danceries (1550) a 4 (3604)

    Phalèse, Pierre: 16th century dances (1583) a 4: 2 vols (3601, 3605)
    Praetorius, Michael: Terpsichore (1612) a 4 (3607): a 5 (3606)
Schott
  Archive series: a large collection of consort music issued separately or
  in small groups of pieces, for instance:
    Holborne, Anthony: Three sets of quintets (50-52)
  Also, in score form:
    Attaingnant, Pierre: Pariser Tanzbuch (1529-30) a 4: 2 vols (3758-9)
    Susato, Tielman: Danserye (1551) a 4: 2 vols (2435-6)

Jacobean consort music
With a wider voice range and more instrumentally conceived, this repertoire
is more suited to players beyond the elementary stage:
  Jacobean Consort Music, ed Dart and Coates, Musica Britannica IX (Stainer
  and Bell) London 1955
    Included are a number of dances in 5 parts. Off-prints, with parts, are
    available.
See also the Schott/Archive series mentioned above.

Piano music
Children's piano music in the style of the works mentioned below can often
be suitably arranged for many combinations of instruments.
    Bartók: Mikrokosmos (6 books), For Children (4 books) and Ten Easy
             Pieces (Boosey)
    Schubert: piano duets - the marches are worth exploring, and other short
             pieces of this genre.
    Schumann: Kinderscenen op 15, Album für die Jugend op 68, and
             Albumblätter op 124
The Children's Folk Songs by Brahms, of which there are a great number with
simple piano accompaniments, should also be considered.

STRING ENSEMBLE
Apart from sources already mentioned, it is worth exploring 17th- and 18th-
century dance suites for keyboard, organ chorale preludes by Pachelbel,
Buxtehude, and Bach, and selected vocal music extracted from, for example,
Handel's operas and oratorios. The following suggestions are made as
pointers to collections, rather than to specific works:
    Bach, J. S. : Book for Anna Magdalena: this contains many simple dances
                   which can be expanded.
    Handel: Aylesford Pieces (Schott 2129a)

Mendelssohn: <u>Songs without words</u>: a number of these piano pieces will
                happily transfer to strings.
Minuets and trios from piano sonatas by Haydn and Mozart.

WOODWIND ENSEMBLE

16th- and early 17th-century canzonas, ricercares, and motets by the
Venetian school - Giovanni Gabrieli and others. There are editions by
Musica Rara, Heugel, and others. Pezel's 'tower music' is published by
Musica Rara.
Polychoral motets by Schütz make excellent arrangements, often dividing
into high and low choirs.
Minuet-Trio movements from early Haydn symphonies.
18th-century chorale preludes by Pachelbel, Buxtehude, and others.

BRASS ENSEMBLE

The early brass repertoire is described above. Some 19th-century music is
equally adaptable, for instance, the Nocturne from Mendelssohn's <u>Midsummer
Night's Dream</u> music. The same composer's organ sonatas are also worth exploring, though these are possibly more suited to the larger forces of the
brass and concert wind band.

JUNIOR ENSEMBLE

The important thing to consider in choosing music for this variable forma-
tion is that harmonic changes should be few. Hence the emphasis which is
placed on traditional folk material, already listed.
Brahms' arrangements of folk songs such as 'Sonntag' (Sunday), 'Wiegenlied'
(Cradle Song) and 'Sandmännchen' (The Little Sandman) are very useful.
Song material in general use in schools can also be adapted.

ORCHESTRA

An obvious source is the repertoire of works for full orchestra, which can
be reduced to suit the forces more likely to be found in schools and youth
groups. Generally speaking it is more profitable to explore music of the
19th century than the symphonic works of the Classical period, which are
over-dependent on clean string playing and are in any case scored for
relatively small forces. Extracts from Grieg, Mendelssohn, and the Russian
school, for instance, are fruitful ground. So are marches and ballet music
in 19th-century French and Italian opera. The more popular pieces can
often be found in piano albums, and piano duet versions of orchestral
scores, dating from before the days of the gramophone, provide a large
repertoire.

BRASS BAND

Pieces should be short, rather than long, and not too allegro in tempo.
Again, the 19th- and early 20th-century style of music is most suitable:
military marches by Schubert, Slavonic Dances by Dvořák, the Alla Marcia
from Sibelius' Karelia Suite and, from Wagner's operas, extracts such as
the Chorale from Die Meistersinger.

Songs from opera and oratorio provide another source: 'O Rest in the Lord',
from Mendelssohn's Elijah, is a typical example of a good tune with a
simple accompaniment. Choruses can also be used. Handel, himself a great
arranger of his own and other composers' music, was not above incorporating
movements from his oratorios into some of his concertos for multiple wind
and strings.

CONCERT WIND BAND

Much that was listed for brass band applies equally here, but the greater
flexibility of the woodwind allows an extended repertoire adapted from
symphonic music. This source is now being covered largely by profession-
ally arranged publications. However, a few suggestions may act as
pointers:

   Berlioz: 'Marche troyenne', from The Trojans
   Berlioz: 'The Hungarian March' and Brander's Song with chorus from
                  The Damnation of Faust
   Bizet: Prelude to Act 1 in Carmen
   Mendelssohn: 'Clowns' Dance' from A Midsummer Night's Dream
   Schubert: movements from the ballet music in Rosamunde

Turning to the 20th century, pieces such as Gershwin's An American in Paris
and selections from Porgy and Bess are obvious possibilities.

SUMMARY

An hour spent in a good public library searching for suitable material is
an hour well spent.

When considering a piece of music for adaptation and arrangement, always
keep in mind the overall range, preferred keys, and musical characteristics of a given combination of instruments — brass ensemble, mixed chamber
group or whatever — and above all, the technical competence of the players.

Index

The following are underlined:

    1) titles of musical works: <u>Black Jack</u> ex 90

    2) cross-references: see <u>articulation</u>

    3) page numbers of a main entry on a topic: bowing <u>14-19</u>

       Note: different types of bowing are separately listed and cross-indexed:

                group staccato (bowing)18-19, 117

                staccato, group (bowing) 18-19, 117

ABBREVIATIONS: cs = case study

                ex = musical extract or example

Printed in England by West Central Printing Co. Ltd., London and Suffolk